The latest Ninja Foodi PossibleCooker Cookbook for Beginners

Recipes for Beginners to Create Fabulous Meals with the Ninja Cooker: 2000 Days of Stress-Free, Delicious Ninja Cooking

By Miles M. Hood

TABLE OF CONTENT

INTRODUCTION

I have always had a deep love for food. In my Italian-Croatian family, Heat day dinner was the most anticipated event of the week when I was growing up. This supper was an occasion more than just a meal. We frequently invited our grandparents, aunts, uncles, and cousins for several-course meals. Simple yet outstanding, the meal was excellent for a large gathering. Big bowls of salad and spaghetti, roasted chicken, and tureens filled with chicken tortellini soup all stick in my memory. Everything was presented in a familial manner. A pot of freshly made coffee and pastries, cakes, or pies were typically served after dinner.

Heatday afternoons were about family, dining together, and joking around the table, even though I've always connected them with food. A good meal can be simple, inexpensive, and fancy. Being delicious without AddPang forth a lot of work is more important. You have more time to share the meal with others when there is less labor.

I have spent years honing my cooking skills. I've always enjoyed reading cookbooks and food publications. However, I never really enjoyed following recipes that called for a long list of ingredients or specific foods to be purchased from a specialist food store. I can tell a recipe isn't for me when I read it and realize it's longer than my son's high school English paper.

Meals with my kids were as fuss-free as possPoundsle when they were little. On most nights, I finished AddPang dinner on the table fast. I had to make brief excursions to the grocery store because I had children. These journeys were uncommon.

I stock up on the necessary items to make quick and straightforward meals.

Growing up, I discovered that meals had to be enjoyable and stress-free. I developed this book to demonstrate how I could make that a reality after learning how to do so. Making stress-free dinners in your kitchen is more straightforward than you might imagine, even if you weren't raised in a household of chefs and have yet to try all my recipes.

In this book, I'll teveryyou how to cook a tonne of delicious meals without a tonne of work. There are several recipes in it, but they all call for at most five essential components, so no extensive grocery lists are needed. There's also little prep. Cooking knowledge is optional to prepare the easy Bowles in this book. You'll have delicious, worry-free dinners if you follow the directions.

The Bowles in this book are not dissimilar from the ones I've enjoyed at those Heatday dinners over the years. Many of them have been adjusted so that, like me, you may still make them when time is of the essence. Cooking should be fun, and these recipes are simple enough for your kids to assist you if you have any. This book contains recipes to help you Add dinner on the table faster than you could go out to grab a takeaway.

FIG & RICOTTA TOAST

Prep Time:5 mins | Total Time:5 mins

INGREDIENTS

- 1 slice crusty whole-grain bread (1/2-inch thick)
- ¼ cup of part-skim ricotta cheese
- 1 fresh fig or 2 dried, sliced
- 1 tsp sliced almonds, toasted
- 1 tsp honey
- Pinch of flaky sea salt, such as Maldon

DIRECTIONS

Toast the bread. Add almonds, figs, and ricotta cheese on top. Season with sea salt and drizzle with honey.

GREEK YOGURT WITH HONEY AND WALNUTS

Prep Time: 10 min | Total Time: 10 min

INGREDIENTS

- 2 1/2 cup ofs of strained Greek yogurt
- 3/4 tsp vanilla extract
- 1 cup of walnuts
- 1/2 of a cup of honey
- cinnamon powder

INSTRUCTIONS

- To make this delectable Greek yogurt dessert with honey, roast the walnuts first. Set oven temperature to 180°CUP OF Arrange the walnuts in a solitary layer on a baking sheet, toasPang for seven to eight minutes or Before they become aromatic and brown. Place in a bowl with the roasted walnuts, then drizzle with the honey and stir to coat. Let it cool for one or two minutes.
- Meanwhile, mix the Greek yogurt and vanilla essence, then divide the mixture among six to seven dessert Bowles. Drizzle the yogurt with the honey-walnut mixture and dust with cinnamon powder.
- Serve right away or keep chilled. Have fun!

MEDITERRANEAN-STYLE CUTFAST QUINOA BOWLS

Prep Time: 5 Mins | Cook Time: 5 Mins

INGREDIENTS

- 2 large eggs
- 2 cup ofs of cooked quinoa
- 3/4 cup of greek yogurt
- 3/4 cup of muhammara
- 3 Ounces baby spinach
- 6 Ounces cherry sliced tomatoes
- 4 Ounces marinated kalamata olives
- 1 lemon, halved
- a pinch of salt & pepper
- heavy drizzles of hot chili oil
- sesame seeds & fresh dill to garnish

DIRECTIONS

- I always poach my eggs using the TasPang Table approach, so that's how you should do it! It functions perfectly.
- Evenly distrPoundsute the quinoa, Greek yogurt, muhammara, baby spinach, tomatoes, and olives in your bowls, leaving space in the middle for the egg. Place a half-lemon (squeezed directly on top) in everybowl and nestle the poached egg inside. Finally, add a sprinkling of salt and pepper and an enormous amount of spicy chili oil (use as much as you like, but I suggest a lot!). Finally, add some sesame seeds and fresh dill as garnish. Consume!

SHAKSHOUKA (POACHED EGGS IN SPICY TOMATO SAUCE)

Yield: 3-4 Servings | Total Time: 45minutes Minutes

INGREDIENTS

- 2 tbsp olive oil
- 1 onion, chopped
- 2 anaheim peppers seeded and chopped
- 1 jalapeño peppers, seeded and finely chopped
- 1 28-ounce can / 794 g diced tomatoes
- ½ cup of / 120 g vegetable broth
- 1 tsp ground cumin
- 1 tsp smoked paprika
- ½ tsp dried oregano
- ½ tsp salt, or to taste
- ¼ tsp freshly ground black pepper, or to taste
- 6-8 eggs
- 2 tbsp chopped fresh parsley
- ¼ cup of / 40 g crumbled feta cheese, for topping
- fresh pita bread, for serving

INSTRUCTIONS

- In a pan, heat the oil over medium-high heat in a big, deep skillet. Add them for about seven minutes, or Before the onion and peppers are soft and starPang to brown.
- When the mixture thickens, cook it for 20 to 22 minutes after adding tomatoes, cumin, paprika, oregano, vegetable broth, salt, and pepper.
- Shake well and crack eggs equally over sauce; cook, covered, for six to eight minutes, or Before the yolks are thick but the whites are still runny (cook an additional minute or two if desired).
- Serve warm pita bread alongside and garnish with feta cheese and parsley.

SIMPLE POACHED EGG AND AVOCADO TOAST

Total Time: 10 Minutes | Yield: 1

INGREDIENTS

- 2 eggs
- 2 slices whole grain bread
- 1/3 avocado (usually I cut it in half but don't use all of it. okay fine maybe I do.)
- 2 tbsp shaved Parmesan cheese
- salt and pepper for topping
- fresh herbs (parsley, thyme, or basil) for topping
- quartered heirloom tomatoes for serving

INSTRUCTIONS

- Heat enough water in a pot to cover the eggs when they are laid in the bottom. Two mason Container lids, with their outside rims only, should be dropped into the pot to lay flat on the bottom. Once the water reaches boiling, please reTransfer it from the heat source and gently crack the eggs into everyrim. Cover the saucepan and poach for five minutes (four for incredPoundsly soft yolks, five minutes or longer for semi-soft yolks).

- Toast the bread and squish the avocado onto everyslice while the eggs fry. When the eggs are finished, reTransfer them from the water using a spatula. Place the poached eggs on top of the toast after gently removing the egg rims (I do this directly on the spatula, over the water). Serve with the freshly quartered heirloom tomatoes and add some salt, Parmesan cheese, and other toppings, such as pepper and fresh herbs.

SIMPLE POACHED EGG AND AVOCADO TOAST

Total Time: 10 Minutes Yield: 1

INGREDIENTS

- 2 eggs
- 2 slices whole grain bread
- 1/3 avocado (usually I cut it in half but don't use all of it. okay fine maybe I do.)
- 2 tbsp shaved Parmesan cheese
- salt and pepper for topping
- fresh herbs (parsley, thyme, or basil) for topping
- quartered heirloom tomatoes for serving

INSTRUCTIONS

- Heat enough water in a pot to cover the eggs when they are laid in the bottom. Two mason Container lids, with their outside rims only, should be dropped into the pot to lay flat on the bottom. Once the water reaches boiling, please reTransfer it from the heat source and gently crack the eggs into everyrim. Cover the saucepan and poach for five minutes (four for incredPoundsly soft yolks, five minutes or longer for semi-soft yolks).

- Toast the bread and squish the avocado onto everyslice while the eggs fry. When the eggs are finished, reTransfer them from the water using a spatula. Place the poached eggs on top of the toast after gently removing the egg rims (I do this directly on the spatula, over the water). Serve with the freshly quartered heirloom tomatoes and Add a dash of salt, Parmesan cheese, pepper, and fresh herbs.

TOMATO & OLIVE TAPENADE BRUSCHETTA

Prep Time : 15 Mins | Cook Time: 20 Mins | Total Time: 35 Mins

INGREDIENTS

- 2 C multi-colored hierloom baby tomatoes - or cherry tomatoes
- good quality olive oil
- ½ C kalamata olives, pitted and quartered
- ¼ C feta, cubed
- ¼ C chopped basil
- 2 Tbsp fresh rosemary, minced
- 1 small loaf artisan bread, sliced
- kosher salt & ground black pepper

INSTRUCTIONS

- Turn the oven on at 425.
- Add parchment paper on the rim of a baking sheet—coat tomatoes with one tbsp of olive oil. Place the tomatoes on a baking sheet and season with kosher salt and pepper. Could you give it a 20-minute roast?
- Mix olives, feta, tomatoes, basil, rosemary, and one tsp of olive oil, followed by salt and pepper for seasoning in a medium-sized bowl. Blend the ingredients Before they are well mixd.
- A giant skillet should be heated at medium-high heat. Halve the bread slices. Swirl around two tbsp of olive oil in the skillet. Add the bread and toast it lightly on both sides. Place the bread on a serving platter, cover it with the olive and tomato tapenade, and proceed to serve.

MEDITERRANEAN-STYLE CUTFAST TOAST

Total Time: 10 Minutes | Yield: 4

INGREDIENTS

- 4 thick slices whole grain or whole wheat bread of choice
- ½ cup of/123 g hummus (homemade or quality store-bought)
- Za'atar spice blend, to your liking
- Handful baby arugula
- 1 cucumber, sliced into rounds
- 1 to 2 Roma tomatoes, sliced into rounds
- 2 tbsp/about 16 g chopped olives of your choice
- Crumbled feta cheese, a sprinkle to your liking

INSTRUCTIONS

- Toasted bread pieces according to the desired texture
- On everyslice of bread, spread around two tbsp of hummus. After adding a healthy pinch of Za'atar spice, pile on the rocket with the additional ingredients. Could you take pleasure in it?

BAKED EGG WITH SPINACH AND FETA

Prep Time:5 minutes | Cook Time:20 minutes | Total Time:25minutes

INGREDIENTS

- 3 tsp olive oil
- 3-4 cup ofs of fresh spinach washed
- 1 whole egg
- 1 ounce crumbled feta
- salt/pepper

INSTRUCTIONS

- Adjust the oven's temperature to 350 degrees Fahrenheit (180 degrees Celsius).
- Sauté spinach in a pan for two to three minutes with one tsp of heated olive oil.
- Add the spinach in a small, heatproof ceramic casserole Bowl, then mix with the remaining two tsp of olive oil.
- Scatter the feta cheese, crack an egg over Season spinach with salt & pepper to taste.
- For roughly 18 to 20 minutes, bake.
- Warm servings are recommended.

OATMEAL WITH DATES & ALMONDS

Prep Time: 10 Minutes | cook Time: 10 Minutes

INGREDIENTS

- 2 tbsp ALMONDS
- 1/4 tsp CARDAMOM
- 1/4 tsp CINNAMON
- 2 whole DATES (DRIED)
- 1 tsp GHEE
- 1 c MILK
- 1/3 c OATS / OATMEAL

INSTRUCTION

- Soak the almonds for the entire night, then peel them the next day.
- Fill a pot with muesli, almonds, and every item on the above list. Use twice or three times as much milk, depending on how dry your body is. If you find milk difficult to digest, try almond milk instead.
- Bring to a boil while conPanuously stirring. Reduce heat to a simmer and let it cook Before soft. Add a sprinkling of cinnamon as garnish.

SMOOTHIE BOWL WITH FRESH BERRIES, NUTS AND SEED

Prep Time: 2 mins | Total Time:2 mins

INGREDIENTS

For the Smoothie:

- 3 cup ofs of mixed berries, frOuncesen
- 2 bananas, sliced, frOuncesen*
- 2 Silk Vanilla Yogurts
- 1/2 cup of Silk Almond Milk

For the Toppings:

- Fresh berries
- Roasted nuts, almonds, walnuts, pecans**
- 1/2 tsp flax seed

INSTRUCTIONS

- Mix the berries, banana slices, yogurt, and milk; purée Before smooth. Pour into two bowls (or, for Cutfast on the go, leave out the topping and pour into a glass or cup of to drink).
- Add flax seed, nuts, and fresh berries on top. Serve right away.

LEMON RICOTTA PANCAKES

Prep Time:10mins | Cook Time: 15mins

INGREDIENTS

- 1 1/2 cup ofs of (214g) all-purpose flour (scoop and level to measure)
- 3 1/2 Tbsp (46g) granulated sugar
- 2 tsp baking powder
- 1/4 tsp baking soda
- 1/2 tsp salt
- 1 cup of (236ml) milk
- 3/4 cup of (180g) ricotta (low-fat or whole)
- 3 large eggs
- 1 tsp vanilla extract
- 1 - 2 Tbsp lemon zest (depending on how lemony you want them)
- 1/4 cup of (60ml) fresh lemon juice
- 1 Tbsp (14g) melted butter

INSTRUCTIONS

- Turn on a medium-high heat on an electric grill or use a nonstick skillet.
- The flour, baking soda, and powdered baking soda should be mixed with a whisk to mix granulated sugar in a mixing Bowl for 20 seconds.
- Create a well in the middle of the flour mixture and reserve.
- Blend the milk, ricotta, eggs, and vanilla thoroughly in a large mixing basin.
- The milk mixture will curdle a little, but that's okay. Incorporate the butter, lemon juice, and zest Before blended.
- Transfer the milk mixture into the combination of flour immediately, whisking only Before mixed (the batter should still have some lumps).
- After adding 1/3 cup of of batter to an oiled skillet or pan, heat it Before bubbles form on the surface and the bottom is golden brown. Then, turn it over and cook the other side Before golden brown.
- Serve warm, topped with berry or maple syrup and, if preferred, a dusPang of powdered sugar.

FRIED HALLOUMI CHEESE WITH CHERRY TOMATOES

Prep Time: 5mins | Total Time: 5mins

INGREDIENTS

- 8 ounces halloumi cheese
- 5-10 cherry tomatoes
- 2 tsp olive oil
- 1 tsp dry oregano

INSTRUCTIONS

- Slice the halloumi in slices about ½ inch thick
- Slice the tomatoes on half.
- Heat the olive oil in a small pan and fry the halloumi for about 2 minutes on everyside Before golden.
- Add the tomatoes when sautéing the other side of the halloumi.
- ReTransfer from the pan and sprinkle the oregano.
- Squeeze a bit of lemon on the cheese before serving.

MEDITERRANEAN TOFU SCRAMBLE

Prep Time:10mins | Cook Time:10mins | Total Time:20mins

INGREDIENTS

For the Mediterranean Tofu Scramble:

- 2 tbsp olive oil
- 1 small red onion diced
- 2 cloves garlic minced
- 1 pound extra-firm tofu drained and pressed at least 15 minutes
- 1 medium red bell pepper diced
- 2 tbsp soy sauce

- 1 tbsp lemon juice
- 1-2 tbsp za'atar seasoning to taste
- 1 tsp ground turmeric
- ½ tsp crushed red pepper flakes
- ¼ cup of finely chopped fresh parsley
- 2-3 green onions chopped

For Serving (optional):

- Toast
- Pita bread
- Hot sauce
- Hummus

INSTRUCTIONS

- Melt olive oil in a big skillet and set it over medium heat. Sauté the onion for around 5 minutes, or Before it softens, once the oil is heated. Sauté the garlic for an additional minute.
- Toss in the bell pepper, tofu crumbles, soy sauce, lemon juice, za'atar, and red pepper flakes in the skillet. After 5 minutes of cooking, turn the pepper pieces with a spatula to ensure they are soft-crisp. Stir in the scallions and parsley once the pan is no longer hot.
- The Bowl would have pita, bread, spicy sauce, and hummus.

APRICOT PORRIDGE

Cooking Time: 10 minutes | Skill Level: Easy | Serves: 1

INGREDIENTS

- 40g Mornflake Scottish Jumbo oats
- 250ml unsweetened almond milk
- ¼ tsp almond extract
- 1 apricot
- Toppings
- 1 apricot
- Small handful of toasted almond flakes or chopped almonds
- Almond butter
- Dark chocolate

METHOD

- Place the oats in a pot after weighing them, and then pour the almond milk on top. Soak the oats for 20 minutes before cooking to make a creamier porridge. After that, toss in 1 sliced apricot and almond extract. Cook the oats in a saucepan of simmering water, stirring occasionally, Before they are soft and creamy.
- Before serving, transfer to a platter and top with apricot slices, almonds (chopped and toasted), almond flakes, almond butter, dark chocolate chips, and a tsp.

CAPRESE AVOCADO TOAST

Prep Time:10mins | Total Time:10mins

INGREDIENTS

- 2 ripe avocados
- 2 tsp fresh lemon juice
- Sea salt and black pepper to taste
- 4 slices bread toasted
- 4 ounces fresh mOunceszarella, sliced and cut into pieces, to fit the bread
- 1 cup of grape tomatoes, halved
- 1/4 cup of basil leaves, roughly chopped
- Balsamic Glaze, for drizzling

INSTRUCTIONS

- In a small bowl, transfer the avocado flesh after halving the fruit and removing the pit—season with a dressing of black pepper, sea salt, and lemon pulp. Mash the ingredients with a fork to retain a slightly chunky texture.
- On top of the toasted bread, evenly distrPoundsute the mashed avocado. Garnish with basil, tomatoes, and slices of fresh mOunceszarella. More salt and pepper can be added if desired. Quickly serve with a drizzle of balsamic glaze.
- I prefer the use of whole-grain bread. Use gluten-free bread if you're trying to make a gluten-free version of this Bowl. You can also use tomato slices instead of grape tomatoes if you like.

MUSHROOM AND SPINACH FRITTATA

Preparation time: 15 min | Cooking Time: 30 min

INGREDIENTS

- 6 eggs
- 1/4 cup of (60 ml) milk
- 1 cup of (250 ml) grated cheddar cheese
- 1 onion, thinly sliced
- 4 Ounces (115 g) white button mushrooms, sliced
- 3 tbsp (45 ml) butter
- 2 cup ofs of (500 ml) baby spinach
- Salt and pepper

PREPARATION

- Adjust the oven's temperature to 180°C or 350°F with the rack in the center position. Grease a square baking Bowl that measures 20 cm (8 inches). ReTransfer from the heat.
- Eggs and milk should be whisked together in a big basin. Sprinkle with cheese. Add salt and pepper to taste. Set the bowl apart.
- Melt the butter in a big nonstick skillet over medium heat and sauté the mushrooms and onion. Add salt and pepper to taste. While stirring regularly, sauté the spinach for another minute.
- Mix the egg mixture with the mushroom mixture. Pour mixture into baking Bowl and mix thoroughly. Lightly brown and puff the frittata in the oven for approximately 25 minutes. Cut the frittata into four equal pieces using a spatula and set everypiece aside. When you Add it on a platter, it's ready to be served either warm or cold.

CHICKPEA CUTFAST HASH WITH SUMMER VEGGIES

Prep Time: 5mins | Cook Time: 15minus | Total Time: 20mins

INGREDIENTS

- 1 tbsp oil
- 1 summer squash or zucchini, sliced into 1/2-inch half moons
- 1 small red onion, sliced into 1/4-inch half moons
- 3 mini sweet peppers, cut into 1/4-inch slices, or 1 bell pepper
- 1 (15 Ounces) can chickpeas drained
- ½ tsp cumin
- ¼ tsp coriander
- ⅛ tsp cinnamon
- ½ tsp salt, + more to taste
- 2 eggs

INSTRUCTIONS

Using a campfire or camp stove, A pan over medium-high heat should be used to heat the oil Before it shimmers. Add the zucchini, onions, peppers, and sauté for about 5 minutes or Before the veggies soften. After adding the drained chickpeas and spices, simmer for ten minutes or Before the vegetables and chickpeas are thoroughly cooked and have some browning on them.

Push the chickpeas and vegetables to the following:

- Push a well in the skillet's center. If the
- The pan dries at the bottom, so add a little oil. Once
- Inside the well, crack two eggs and cook Before desired.
- After
- Take the skillet from the heat and Add it on the table.

SUMMER BERRY PARFAIT WITH YOGURT AND GRANOLA

Prep Time:10 mins | Total Time:10 mins | Servings:1

INGREDIENTS

- ¾ cup of sliced strawberries
- ¾ cup of blueberries
- 1 (6 ounce) container vanilla yogurt
- 1 tbsp wheat germ
- ½ banana, sliced
- ⅓ cup of granola

DIRECTIONS

- Prepare a big bowl by layering 1/4 cup of of strawberries,
- 1/4 cup of of blueberries,
- 1/3 container of yogurt,
- 1/3 tbsp of wheat germ,
- 1/3 of the sliced banana,
- and approximately two tbsp of granola.
- Keep building the parfait by layering the ingredients Before you've used them all.

BAGEL WITH CREAM CHEESE AND SMOKED SALMON

10 mins to prepare and 10 mins to cook

INGREDIENTS

- 4 white seeded bagels, halved horizontally
- 100g smoked salmon slices
- 1 tbsp lemon juice
- 150g cream cheese
- 1 tsp chives, finely chopped, stalks to garnish

METHOD

- Bring both halves of the bagel to a golden brown toast. At the same time, in a small bowl, mix the lemon juice and smoked salmon. Spread half of the toasted bagels with softened cream cheese, which you may do in a mixing Bowl using a spoon.
- On top of the cream cheese, distrPoundsute the smoked salmon slices evenly. Top with chopped chives. Place on designated serving platters.
- Top the smoked salmon with a few chive stalks and set aside the toasted top halves of the bagels. Make sure to serve right away.

Prep Time: 5mins | Cook Time: 25mins

INGREDIENTS

- 2 tbsp bacon grease
- 1 medium sweet onion, finely diced
- 1 clove garlic, minced
- 4 cup ofs of chicken broth
- 1 (28-ounce) can petite diced tomatoes, undrained
- 2 cup ofs of long grain white rice
- 1/2 tsp salt

INSTRUCTIONS

- The bacon fat should be melted over medium-high heat in a big saucepan with a lid that fits snugly. Toss in the onions and sauté Before they become soft and transparent. After one minute, add the garliCup of
- Toss in the tomatoes and chicken broth. Heat till boiling. Include the rice and mix thoroughly. TasPang salt is optional. Turn the heat down to low and simmer, covered. Once the vegetables are soft and the liquid absorbed, cook for another 20 to 25 minutes. After the rice has rested for five more minutes, please turn off the heat so it can absorb any remaining liquid. Before serving, use a fork to fluff the rice.

FUSILLI WITH BROCCOLI AND ANCHOVIES

Total Time: 30 mins

INGREDIENTS

- 1generous bunch broccoli (about 1¾ pounds)
- Salt and black pepper
- 1pound fusilli pasta
- 3tbsp extra-virgin olive oil
- 2garlic cloves, minced
- 4 to 5anchovy fillets rinsed and chopped
- ½tsp red pepper flakes
- Freshly grated Parmesan or pecorino, for serving

PREPARATION

- Get a big saucepan of water boiling. ReTransfer the broccoli heads from their stems, reserving the thick stems for another use; leave a 1-inch stem at the bottom of everyhead.
- Add broccoli to boiling water and season with salt. For around five or six minutes, boil or Before fork-soft.
- Skip-draining the water and transferring broccoli crowns to a basin of cold water using a slotted spoon, skimmer, or tongs. Blot the broccoli after draining it. Finely chop.
- Then, add the fusilli and return the water to a boil.
- Toss in the garlic, anchovies, and red pepper flakes (if using) with two tbsp of olive oil and sauté the fusilli in a large, heavy skillet over medium heat. Swirl and mash the anchovies with a wooden spoon for approximately one minute and cook Before aromatiCup of Blend in the broccoli florets.
- Toss the broccoli with a couple of spoons, or around half a cup of, of the pasta water. Add salt and pepper according to taste. Cook, stirring occasionally, over medium heat for five minutes. Make sure the broccoli is soft. Reserve the pasta water by removing it with a second spoon.

- Mix the drained pasta, broccoli, and remaining olive oil and toss to mix. Add the water you set aside if you think it needs more moisture. Garnish with cheese and serve immediately.

FARRO WITH SPINACH AND MUSHROOMS

Prep Time: 10 Minutes | Cook Time: 15 Minutes | Total Time: 25 Minutes

INGREDIENTS

- 4 cup ofs of farro, cooked (~ 2 cup ofs of dry)
- 2 tbsp olive oil
- 1/2 red onion, thinly sliced (about 1 cup of)
- 8 Ounces crimini mushrooms, thinly sliced
- 1 1/2 tbsp (5 cloves) minced garlic
- 1/2 tsp dried thyme
- 2 cup ofs of baby spinach, packed
- 1/4 tsp red pepper flakes (or more)
- salt + pepper to taste
- 1/4 cup of dried tart cherries
- 2 tbsp parmesan cheese

INSTRUCTIONS

- Toss the red onions with one tbsp of olive oil and sauté them for 3 to 4 minutes in a medium skillet over medium heat, stirring occasionally to prevent browning. Transfer the onions to a separate small Bowl and set them aside.
- Add one tbsp of olive oil after the garlic and mushrooms have been sautéed for three to four minutes. Mix with the dried thyme, young spinach, and red pepper flakes. Keep cooking for another three minutes or Before the spinach wails slightly. Stir in the red onions, farro, sour cherries, parmesan, salt, and pepper. Make sure to heat everything. Keep heated before serving.

PASTA CARBONARA WITH TURKEY BACON AND PEAS

Prep Time: 18mins | Cook Time: 20mins | Total Time:38mins

INGREDIENTS

- 1 lb. spaghetti
- 1 Tbsp. extra-virgin olive oil
- 3/4 lb. turkey bacon sliced into 1/4-inch pieces
- 1 cup of fr0uncesen peas
- 2 cloves garlic minced
- 4 eggs
- 1/4 tsp. salt optional
- 1/4 tsp. freshly ground black pepper
- 1/2 cup of grated Parmesan cheese + additional for garnish
- 1/2 Tbsp. dried parsley optional
- fresh parsley sprigs for garnish optional

INSTRUCTIONS

- Over high heat, bring one tbsp of salt and 1 gallon of water to a boil in a big saucepan. Pasta should be added to boiling water. Around 8 to 9 minutes of cooking time is required for al dente.
- Add oil in a big nonstick skillet and set it over medium-high heat while water is boiling. Include turkey bacon. Stir often and cook for approximately 4 minutes or Before it browns. Blend in the peas. It may take 2–3 minutes for the peas to boil and for the bacon to brown completely; remember that turkey bacon, unlike pork bacon, will caramelize slightly rather than crisp completely. Simmer for one more minute after adding the garlic another minute, or Before it becomes golden. Take off the stove.
- In a big bowl, whisk together the eggs, pepper, Parmesan cheese, salt (if using), and pasta while it cooks. After the spaghetti is cooked, strain it in a colander and set aside 1/4 cup of of the cooking water. They Transfer the pasta to the bowl using tongs with the egg mixture. Add the pasta water and stir to blend, allowing the eggs to cook in the pasta's heat. Mix the peas and turkey bacon; stir

to mix. Finally, top with a little Parmesan and dried parsley, if desired. If desired, top with a sprig of parsley and serve right away.

PASTA WITH PARMESAN AND GARLIC ZUCCHINI

Prep Time: 10 Mins | Cook Time: 20 Mins | Total Time: 30 Mins

INGREDIENTS

- 3 tbsp olive oil
- 4 zucchinis medium, sliced
- 4 garlic cloves , minced
- 8 ounces spaghetti (for gluten free version, use brown rice pasta spaghetti style)
- salt and pepper
- 1 cup of Parmesan cheese freshly shredded

INSTRUCTIONS

- Get the olive oil hot in a big skillet over medium-high heat. Sauté the minced garlic and sliced zucchini for 5-7 minutes, turning periodically, Before the zucchini softens and browns slightly, without cover. Add salt halfway through cooking.
- Be aware that you may need to cook the zucchini in two batches, depending on the size of your skillet.
- Pasta recipes call for certain cooking times. To stop the pasta from cooking, drain and rinse it with cold water.
- Toss in the cooked pasta while the garlic and zucchini are cooking over low heat.
- Toss in some freshly grated Parmesan and toss the pasta in the skillet over low heat Before the cheese melts. Spice it up with some salt and pepper.

PENNE PASTA WITH FETA AND SUMMER VEGETABLES

Ready In:25mins

INGREDIENTS

- 100ml olive oil
- 1garlic clove crushed
- 200g zucchini juliene
- 200g black olives
- 1/2red capsicum chopped
- 1/2yellow capsicum chopped
- 500g cherry tomatoes halved
- 150g feta cheese, crumbled
- 1tbsp thyme
- 500g penne pasta or 500 g pasta of choice

DIRECTIONS

- Saute the pasta in boiling water Before it reaches the desired doneness, al dente. Pour off any excess oil and set aside.
- Fry the garlic, zucchini, and both capsicums in olive oil over high heat for two or three minutes, stirring occasionally, Before the vegetables are soft.
- Cook for a Another 30 seconds after incorporaPang the tomatoes.
- Next, mix the herbs, olives, and feta cheese.
- Cook for a Another minute before adding seasonings.
- Top with chopped herbs, and toss the pasta with the cheese and veggie combination.

CREAMY HEAT-DRIED TOMATO PESTO PASTA WITH CHICKEN

Prep Time: 10 minutes | Cook Time: 30 minutes | Total Time: 40 minutes

INGREDIENTS

For the heat-dried tomato pesto:

- 1/2 cup of heat dried tomatoes packed in oil
- 1/2 cup of fresh basil
- 2 cloves garlic
- 1/4 cup of parmigiano reggiano (parmesan cheese) grated
- 1/4 cup of olive oil (or oil from heat dried tomatoes)
- salt and pepper to taste

For the pasta:

- 8 ounces pasta (gluten-free for gluten-free)
- 4 ounces bacon, cut into small pieces (optional)
- 2 tbsp butter
- 1 pound boneless skinless chicken breasts or thighs, cut into bite sized pieces
- salt and pepper to taste (or cajun seasoning) – link this
- 2 cloves garlic, chopped
- 2 tbsp flour
- 1 cup of chicken broth
- 1 cup of heavy/whipping cream (or milk)
- 1/2 tsp oregano
- 1/2 cup of heatdried tomato pesto (see above)
- 1/4 cup of parmigiano reggiano (parmesan cheese), grated
- 2 cup ofs of baby spinach (optional)

DIRECTIONS

- Blend all of the ingredients for the pesto with heat-dried tomatoes Before smooth.
- **Pasta:** Start cooking the pasta per the instructions on the package.
- After the bacon has been cooked Before crispy, please reTransfer it from the pan and pat it dry using paper towels.
- Add the chicken to the melted butter in a large pan over medium heat—season with salt and pepper to taste. Toss the chicken around occasionally while cooking Before it gets a bit brown and cooked through, which should take approximately 7 to 10 minutes.

- Cook, stirring occasionally, for approximately one minute, Before garlic is aromatic, then add flour and conPanue cooking.
- Bring the broth, cream, and oregano to simmer after bringing it to a boil for three minutes or Before the sauce is slightly thickened.
- After adding the pesto and parmesan, reduce the stovetop temperature and keep cooking Before the cheese melts into the sauce.
- After combining the bacon and spinach, stir and simmer for a minute or two or Before the spinach has wilted.

SPINACH WALNUT PESTO

Prep Time: 15 mins | Total Time:15 mins | Servings: 4

INGREDIENTS

- 2 cup ofs of fresh baby spinach, stems re Transferd
- 1 cup of freshly grated Parmesan cheese
- 1 cup of fresh parsley chopped leaves
- ½ cup of chopped walnuts
- ¼ cup of water
- 3 cloves garlic
- ¼ tsp salt, or more to taste
- ⅛ tsp ground black pepper
- ½ cup of extra-virgin olive oil

DIRECTIONS

- Blend the ingredients in a food processor: spinach, Parmesan cheese, parsley, walnuts, water, garlic, salt, and pepper. While processing, gradually add oil Before a smooth paste forms.

FARFALLE WITH PROSCIUTTO, SPINACH, PINE NUTS, AND RAISINS

Yield:4

INGREDIENTS

- 1/2 cup of pine nuts
- 1/2 cup of raisins
- 1/2 cup of boiling water
- 1/2 cup of olive oil
- 6 cloves garlic, minced
- 10 ounces spinach, large stems reTransferd, leaves washed and cut crosswise into 1-inch strips
- 1 pound farfalle
- 1/4 pound sliced prosciutto, cut crosswise into 1/4-inch strips
- 1/2 tsp salt
- 1/2 tsp fresh-ground black pepper
- 1/3 cup of grated Parmesan

DIRECTIONS

- Toast the pine nuts for approximately 5 minutes, stirring often, over reasonably low heat in a small frying pan. They should turn golden brown. Alternatively, you might bake them for 5–10 minutes at 350°.
- Bring the water to a boil and add the raisins. After 10 minutes, the fruit should be pliable. Run off.
- Bring the oil to a simmer in a big skillet. While stirring, cook for 1 minute after adding the garliCup of After 2 minutes of tossing, add the spinach and cook Before it wilts a little.
- Cook the farfalle for approximately 15 minutes in a boiling saucepan of salted water. Run off. Pine nuts, raisins, spinach mixture, prosciutto, salt, pepper, and Parmesan should be mixed in.

BARILLA WHOLE GRAIN SPAGHETTI WITH CHERRY TOMATOES AND BASIL

Total time: 12 min | Prep time: 4 min | Cook time: 8 min

INGREDIENTS

- 1 box BARILLA Whole Grain Spaghetti
- 1 clove garlic
- 2 tsp extra virgin olive oil
- 1 pint cherry tomatoes halved
- Salt to taste
- Fresh cracked black pepper to taste
- 5-6 leaves basil, sliced into thin strips
- 1/2 cup of Parmesan grated cheese

DIRECTIONS

- Always follow the package directions for cooking pasta.
- AT THE SAME TIME, heat the olive oil in a big skillet and sauté the minced garlic Before it turns a bit yellow. Saute for 2 minutes after adding cherry tomatoes. After adding salt and pepper, take it off the fire.
- SQUEEZE off any excess water from the pasta and set aside 1/2 cup of.
- Mix 1 cup of of basil, two cloves of garlic, and three cherry tomatoes with the spaghetti. Return pasta to skillet and add leftover cooking liquid; toss to mix.
- Season with black pepper, sprinkle with grated Parmesan, then top with the rest of the basil. □

MEDITERRANEAN ORZO SALAD RECIPE

 Prep Time: – 10MINS | Cook Time: – 10 Mins

INGREDIENTS

- 1 ½ cup of dry orzo pasta
- 1 pint grape or cherry tomatoes, halved
- 2 green onions, trimmed and chopped (both white and green parts)
- ½ green bell pepper, seeds reTransferd chopped
- 1 cup of packed chopped fresh parsley, about 1 ½ ounces
- ½ cup of packed chopped fresh dill, about 0.5 ounces
- ¼ cup of sliced pitted kalamata olives, about 1 ounce
- 2 tsp capers
- Feta cheese, to your liking

For The Dressing:

- 1 lemon, zested and juiced
- ¼ cup of extra virgin olive oil
- 1 garlic clove, minced
- 1 tsp oregano

INSTRUCTIONS

- Prepare the orzo pasta as directed on the packaging; it took approximately 8 minutes. Leave to cool for a little.
- Add all ingredients (except the feta) into a big bowl and toss in the bell peppers, green onions, capers, parsley, dill, olives, and grape tomatoes. Toss in the orzo pasta.
- Get the dressing ready. Whisk together the lemon zest, juice, extra-virgin olive oil, garlic, oregano, and a generous sprinkling of season with black pepper and kosher salt in a small Bowl. Mix by whisking.
- After you pour the dressing over the salad, toss it Before everything is well-coated, especially the orzo pasta.

- Crumble some tangy feta cheese on top. Chill for a few minutes before serving, covered.

SEAFOOD AND GARLIC LINGUINE

Prep Time : 5 Mins | Cook Time:15 Mins

INGREDIENTS

- 250 gm linguine pasta
- 3 tbsp olive oil
- 4 garlic cloves, finely chopped
- 6 anchovies, roughly chopped
- 1 tbsp capers, roughly chopped
- chilli flakes, to your taste
- 8 prawns
- 1 squid bowle, cut into rings
- 1/2 cup of white wine (pinot gris)
- 1.5 tbsp tomato paste
- 1/8 tsp salt or to taste
- pepper, to taste
- 6 cherry tomatoes halved
- Garnish
- 2 lemon wedges
- 3 sprigs parsley leaves, finely chopped (without the stem)

INSTRUCTIONS

- Get everything you need ready.
- The packaging directions should be followed when cooking pasta.
- Toss the garlic and olive oil into a skillet that has been chilled. After the garlic has been infused, reduce the heat to medium.
- After about three and a half minutes, when the garlic begins to bubble, add the anchovies, capers, and chili flakes, if desired. Simmer the anchovies in the oil for a few minutes after mashing them with a wooden spoon.

- When the pasta is almost done, around 80% done, it's ready to be checked. If yes, conPanue to the following step. Alternatively, take the pan off the stove and let the pasta cook for a little longer.
- Add the squid and prawns in the frying pan and raise the heat to medium-high. After 30 seconds, reTransfer from heat.
- Incorporate the tomato paste, wine, salt, and pepper. Thicken by stirring. (Add additional tomato paste if sauce seems too thin.)
- Add the cooked pasta onto the skillet without draining it first. Use wooden spoons to mix everything.
- Toss the tomatoes gently and taste to adjust the seasoning. Find the right setPang for you.
- Spoon onto individual Bowles and garnish with a squeeze of lemon juice.
- Before serving, garnish with parsley.

GARLIC SHRIMP AND ASPARAGUS RISOTTO

Prep Time: 20 mins | Cook Time: 35 mins | Total Time: 55 mins

INGREDIENTS

- 1 (32 ounce) container chicken broth
- 2 tbsp olive oil
- ⅓ onion, chopped
- ½ clove garlic, minced
- 3 cup ofs of Arborio rice
- 1 pound raw shrimp, peeled and deveined
- 1 pound fresh asparagus, cut into thirds
- ½ cup of grated Parmesan cheese
- 3 tbsp butter
- 1 tbsp salt
- 1 tbsp ground black pepper
- 1 tbsp chopped fresh parsley

DIRECTIONS

- Simmer the chicken stock in a saucepan over medium-low heat after pouring the broth into the pot.
- Meanwhile, place a big saucepan over medium heat and add the olive oil. In heated oil, sauté the garlic and onion for around 2 minutes or Before they soften slightly. Cook the Arborio rice for approximately 4 minutes, stirring often, Before it is coated with oil.
- After the chicken stock has heated through, stir in 1/2 cup of to the pot while stirring conPanuously for around 2 minutes in the pan or Before the rice absorbs the broth. About 15 minutes later, after the first four cycles, conPanue stirring conPanuously Before the rice is creamy, soft, and slightly firm to the bite.
- Add the shrimp and asparagus to the cooked stock and stir to mix. After 2–3 minutes, the shrimp should begin to turn pink. Let the broth cool down.
- Add the shrimp and asparagus to the rice using a slotted spoon. Cook, stirring occasionally, for 1 minute. After the rice has cooked for around a minute, stir in the butter and Parmesan cheese. Take rice out of the heat. Add salt and pepper to taste. Top off every plate with a sprinkle of parsley.

MEDITERRANEAN TUNA PASTA SALAD

Prep Time: 5 mins | Cook Time: 10 mins | Total Time: 15 mins

INGREDIENTS

- 8 ounces fusilli pasta or other small pasta noodles
- ¼ cup of red onion, sliced very thin and chopped small
- 1/2 cup of olive oil
- 1/4 cup of red wine vinegar
- 2 tbsp fresh lemon juice
- 4 cloves garlic, minced
- 2 tsp Za'atar seasoning mix
- 1 tsp kosher salt, adjust to taste
- 1 tsp fresh black pepper, adjust to taste
- 10-12 ounces tuna in water, (2) 5-ounce cans, well-drained

- 6 ounce can whole black olives, drained and halved
- 16 ounces grape tomatoes, sliced in half, about 2 cup ofs of worth
- 1 English cucumber, chopped into 1/2" pieces, about 1 cup of worth
- 1/4 cup of fresh Italian parsley, chopped small
- 1/2 cup of feta, optional

INSTRUCTIONS

- Bring one tbsp of kosher salt and enough water to boil in a large saucepan. Make sure you follow the directions on the pasta package for cooking it. Pasta should be drained without rinsing.
- Transfer the red onion to a medium-sized bowl and mix with the vinegar, lemon juice, olive oil, garlic, Za'atar seasoning, salt, and pepper. Set aside while the pasta cooks. While you're AddPang together the remainder of the salad, stir and set aside.
- Toss the tuna, cooked pasta, olives, tomatoes, and cucumber in a big bowl. Along with the onion, stir in all of the bowl's liquids. Coat everything with the dressing by stirring.
- Add a fair amount of parsley and mix once more. If desired, sprinkle with Feta. If you think the salad needs extra salt or pepper, taste it. When you're ready to eat, serve it or Add it in the fridge. Savor it!

PASTA WITH ROASTED RED PEPPERS AND GOAT CHEESE

Total Time:10 minutes

INGREDIENTS

FOR THE PASTA WITH ROASTED RED PEPPERS AND GOAT CHEESE:

- 2tbsp extra virgin olive oil
- 2garlic cloves, minced
- 1cup of thinly sliced roasted sweet red peppers
- Salt
- freshly ground pepper
- 4large basil leaves, cut in slivers chiffonade optional
- 3ounces goat cheese, crumbled
- ¾pound pasta, any shape

PREPARATION

AS FOR THE GOAT CHEESE AND ROASTED RED PEPPER PASTA

- The first step is to boil a large kettle of water. At the same time, in a big, heavy skillet, warm the olive oil in a medium-sized pan. Toss in the garliCup of While stirring, cook for approximately 30 seconds or Before the mixture smells good. After roughly a minute of mixing, add the roasted peppers, slices, and others, and make sure the peppers are coated with oil and garliCup of Toss in the goat cheese and basil (if using) after seasoning with salt and pepper. Cut off the heat.
- Season the water with salt, then add the pasta when it boils. Prepare the pasta according to the package's instructions Before firm to the biPang or al dente. Pour approximately 1/4 cup of of the pasta cooking water into the skillet and mix thoroughly to melt the goat cheese. Once the pasta is drained, stir it with the pepper mixture immediately in the pan. Take a seat.

BAKED FETA AND TOMATO PASTA

Prep Time: 10 Mins | Cook Time:30 Mins

INGREDIENTS

- 8 Ounces Greek feta cheese
- 2 lbs gourmet medley tomatoes
- ⅓ cup of extra virgin olive oil
- 4-5 garlic cloves halved or quartered if too big
- 2-3 fresh sage leaves
- 2-3 fresh thyme sprigs
- 1-2 rosemary sprigs
- 1 tbsp dry oregano
- 1 tbsp red pepper flakes
- freshly ground pepper
- sea salt

For serving

- fresh basil leaves
- parmesan cheese
- 8 Ounces pasta of your choice. I used penne.

EQUIPMENT

- 11" x 8" baking pan

INSTRUCTIONS

- Bring the oven to a temperature of 190 degrees Celsius, or 375 degrees Fahrenheit.
- In the middle of the baking Bowl, set the feta block. Place the garlic cloves and tomatoes in a circular pattern around the feta. Intersperse the garlic and tomatoes with the thyme, sage, and rosemary sprigs.
- DistrPoundsute the olive oil evenly over the ingredients. Be sure to sprinkle on some freshly ground pepper and a tbsp of oregano.

- Cook in the oven for 30–35 minutes.
- Bring the pasta to a precise al dente texture. Substitute one minute for the stated boiling time in most cases.
- If you need it later, Submerge the pasta in 1 cup of of water and reserve it.
- Take the baking Bowl out of the oven. Add three-quarters of the basil leaves right away. Mash the feta into a smooth sauce by whisking the ingredients together.
- Pasta should be added.
- Toss the pasta gently to coat it evenly.
- If necessary, thin it out a bit and add some creaminess by adding around 1/4 cup of of the reserved pasta water.
- Spoon into individual Bowles and garnish with grated parmesan, chopped fresh basil, and a dash of red pepper flakes.

LINGUINE WITH CLAMS IN WHITE WINE SAUCE

Prep Time: 5mins | Cook Time: 20mins

INGREDIENTS

- 1 lb linguine
- 1 tbsp olive oil
- 3 cloves garlic finely minced
- 1/4 tsp Kosher salt
- 1/4 tsp freshly ground black pepper
- 3/4 cup of white wine
- 1 cup of clam stock
- 1/4 tsp red chili flakes or red chile paste add more if you really like kick
- 3-4 lbs Littleneck or Manila clams (choose amount depending on how much you love clams!)
- 2 tbsp butter
- 1/2 cup of Italian flat-leaf parsley chopped

INSTRUCTIONS

- Heat a big saucepan of water Before it boils. Cook the linguine Before it is barely al dente and season with Kosher salt. After draining, set away.
- Get the olive oil hot in a big skillet over medium-high heat. Sauce, salt, and pepper should be added after the garlic is cooked for a minute or two or Before golden.
- After adding the wine, clam stock, and chile flakes/paste, reduce the liquid for approximately three minutes.
- Once the clams have opened, add them while reducing heat to a simmer for eight to ten minutes with the lid on. Any claims that still need to be opened should be tossed aside.
- Mix the butter and parsley, then stir. Then, Add in the linguine.

FUSILLI WITH CHICKEN, OLIVES, ARTICHOKE, RED PEPPERS AND BASIL

Prep time: 10 minutes | Cook time: 20 minutes

INGREDIENTS

- 200g fusilli
- 250g chicken thighs, skin off and sliced
- 50ml white wine
- 60g kalamata olives
- 60g artichoke hearts
- 60g roasted red peppers, sliced
- olive oil
- 1/2 bunch fresh basil
- parmesan to serve
- salt and pepper to taste

DIRECTIONS

- Get a large kettle of water boiling first and add salt.
- Saute the sliced chicken for 7-8 minutes in a big skillet with two tsp of olive oil over high heat—season with salt after that.
- Toss the pasta into the boiling water to cook while the chicken cooks.
- Before adding the roasted peppers, artichokes, and olives, deglaze the pan with white wine after the chicken turns color.
- Drain the pasta and toss it with the chicken and remaining ingredients once cooked. Before turning off the heat, toss in the basil. Garnish with freshly grated parmesan. Toss in a little more fresh basil and a little more olive oil.

EASY ORZO WITH SHRIMP AND FETA

Prep Time:10 Mins | Cook Time: 15 Mins |Total Time:25 Mins

INGREDIENTS

- 1 cup of uncooked orzo pasta
- 12 jumbo shrimps, peeled and deveined
- 1 tsp Old Bay Seasoning
- 2 tbsp butter
- ½ cup of good quality feta cheese crumbles
- lemon juice to taste
- chopped parsley and lemon wedges to garnish

INSTRUCTIONS

- Pasta should be cooked in salted water according to the directions on the package. ReTransfer excess water, wash with ice water, and set aside. As the shrimp are drying, mix them with the Old Bay Seasoning.
- Add one tbsp of butter into a big Butter; it melts when melted in a nonstick skillet over medium-high heat. Toss in the shrimp and cook on everyside for a minute or two or Before opaque.

- Add the shrimp aside after taking them out of the pan. Please keep the same pan and heat the remaining one tsp of butter Before the color becomes light brown. Serve with orzo and crumbled feta. After thoroughly mixing, reTransfer from heat.
- Top with the prawns and generously sprinkle with lemon juice.
- For garnish, serve with additional feta cheese, lemon wedges, and chopped parsley.

WHOLE WHEAT PENNE IN FRESH TOMATO SAUCE

INGREDIENTS

- 250g Donna Pastaia Whole Wheat Spaghetti
- 4 cup ofs of ripe tomatoes, diced
- 4 cloves of garlic, minced
- 1 small onion, finely chopped
- 1/4 cup of fresh basil leaves, chopped
- 3 tbsp extra virgin olive oil
- 1 tsp dried oregano
- Salt and pepper to taste
- Grated Parmesan cheese (for serving)
- Fresh basil leaves (for garnish)

INSTRUCTIONS

To cook the Whole Wheat Spaghetti:

- Add enough salted water to a large saucepan and bring it to a boil.
- After adding the whole wheat spaghetti, cook it Before it's al dente, following the instructions on the package.
- Save a Pany cup of of the pasta water after draining the noodles.

Get the tomato basil sauce ready. The extra virgin olive oil should be heated in a big skillet in a medium-sized pan. Sauté the diced onion and minced garlic after adding them Before the garlic is fragrant and the onion turns translucent. Add the dried oregano, salt, pepper, and diced tomatoes. Once the tomatoes have broken down and released their juices, stir the sauce well and simmer for 15 to 20 minutes.

Blend the Sauce (Optional): Add the tomato combination in a food processor or blender and process Before the appropriate consistency is reached for a smoother sauce. Add the sauce back in the skillet.

Stir in the freshly chopped basil leaves into the tomato sauce, setPang aside a few for garnish. Add Fresh Basil and Mix with Pasta. Cooked whole wheat spaghetti should be added to the skillet and gently tossed to cover the pasta in a flavorful sauce. If necessary, thin the sauce with some pasta water you set aside.

Present and Garnish: Spoon the Whole Wheat Spaghetti with Tomato Basil Sauce onto bowls or serving plates. Sprinkle-grated Parmesan cheese and finely cut basil leaves on top for an additional taste boost.

Serving and Presentation Ideas:

For extra nutrients and texture, serve this healthy pasta meal with sautéed veggies like spinach, bell peppers, or zucchini.

Pair it with a crisp green salad prepared in a mild vinaigrette to make a well-balanced supper.

To enhance the taste of the tomato basil sauce, pair it with a glass of medium-bodied red wine, like Chianti or Barbera.

If you want a little kick of spice, top the spaghetti with some red pepper flakes.

To finish the meal, serve with crusty whole wheat bread or garlic toast.

This pasta meal is filling and soothing because of the vivid flavors of the tomato basil sauce paired with our whole-grain spaghetti. Savour every mouthful of this hearty and filling Bowl, letPang the simplicity of the ingredients do the talking.

ORZO PASTA SALAD WITH FETA AND HEAT DRIED TOMATOES

Prep Time: 10 Minutes | Cook Time: 8 Minutes | Total Time: 18 Minutes

INGREDIENTS

- 2 qt water
- ½ tsp salt
- 1 lb orzo pasta
- ½ lb kalamata olives, pitted and chopped
- ½ cup of diced red onion
- 12 Ounces heat dried tomatoes, packed in oil, drained and chopped
- 1 cup of thinly sliced spinach
- 3 TBS thinly sliced fresh basil
- 3 TBS thinly sliced fresh mint
- ½ tsp ground black pepper
- 3 TBS extra virgin olive oil
- 3 TBS lemon juice
- ⅓ lb crumbled feta cheese

INSTRUCTIONS

- Bring the water and salt to a boil in a heavy-based saucepan.
- Add the orzo and cook once the water reaches a boiling point as directed on the package.
- Mix the olives, onions, heat-dried tomatoes, spinach, basil, and mint in a sizable serving bowl while the orzo cooks.
- After cooking the pasta, Transfer it to a serving bowl and thoroughly drain it in a strainer. Blend thoroughly.
- Toss gently to mix the remaining ingredients, then serve chilled or at room temperature.

GARLIC-LEMON SHRIMP LINGUINE

Prep/Total Time: 30 min.

INGREDIENTS

- 8 ounces uncooked linguine
- 2 tbsp olive oil
- 1 tbsp butter
- 1 pound uncooked shrimp (26-30 per pound), peeled and deveined
- 3 garlic cloves, minced
- 1 tbsp grated lemon zest
- 1 tbsp lemon juice
- 1 tsp lemon-pepper seasoning
- 2 tbsp minced fresh parsley

DIRECTIONS

Cook the linguine al dente as directed on the packet. In the meantime, warm the butter and oil in a big skillet over medium-high heat. Stir and cook the shrimp for three minutes. Add the garlic, zest, juice, and lemon-pepper spice. Cook and stir for two to three minutes or Before the shrimp turns pink. Add the parsley and stir.

After draining:

- Save one-third of the pasta water.
- Add enough pasta water for the shrimp mixture to have the proper consistency.
- Accompany with linguine.

FARFALLE WITH SPINACH, PINE NUTS, AND GOAT CHEESE.

INGREDIENTS

- 1 box Farfalle pasta
- 1 16 ounce package frOuncesen Cut-Leaf Spinach, defrosted
- 4 Tbsp Butter
- 1 Shallot, diced fine
- 1 Tbsp Garlic, minced
- 3/4 cup of Feta cheese
- 1/4 cup of Parmesan Cheese
- 1 1.75 ounce bottle Pine Nuts (about 1/2 cup of)
- Crushed Red Pepper (optional)

DIRECTIONS

- Cook pasta according to package directions Before it's al dente. While the pasta cooks, get the other ingredients ready. The pine nuts should be lightly browned after 3 to 4 minutes of cooking in a small pan over medium heat. Add the pine nuts aside. Using a cheesecloth or your hands, squeeze out as much moisture as possPoundsle from the spinach. After the pasta is done, drain and reserve. Add the butter in the pasta pot and heat it over medium heat. Stir in the garlic and shallots. Simmer for a little moment. Stir in the spinach after draining it. Incorporate the cheese. Stir and cook for a few minutes or Before the cheese melts into the spinach mixture. Stir in the pine nuts and heated pasta. Mix by tossing. If desired, add some crushed red pepper to season. Serve immediately, Add in the fridge, or sit at room temperature for a few hours.

PESTO PASTA WITH GRILLED CHICKEN, CHERRY TOMATOES AND ARUGULA

Prep Time: 20mins | Cook Time: 20mins | Total Time: 40mins

INGREDIENTS

For the pesto

- 50g/2 ½cup ofs of fresh basil
- 50g/1/3cup of blanched almonds
- 50g/1/3 cup of Grana Padano or Parmesan cheese + extra for serving
- 4 tbsp extra virgin olive oil
- 1 lemon, juice only
- 1 clove garlic

For the Pesto Pasta

- 2 skinless, boneless chicken breasts
- salt
- pepper
- 1 tsp dried basil
- 1 lbs short pasta
- 1 tbsp olive oil
- 2-3 cloves garlic
- 10 cherry tomatoes + a handful more for serving(optional)
- 20g/1cup of rocket/arugula

INSTRUCTIONS

- Add the almonds, squeezed garlic clove, Grana Padano or Parmesan cheese, and one lemon juice in a food processor or blender. Blend Before silky. Add the olive oil using a funnel and wait 10 to 20 seconds while the food processor's motor is still running. Turn off the food processor and taste the pesto; add a little tsp of salt if needed.

- Pasta should be cooked in a big pot of salted water as directed on the package.
- Warm up the barbeque and prepare on everyside for 5 to 7 minutes, depending on the chicken breasts' size and thickness, while the pasta cooks. Salt and pepper should be used to season the chicken breasts, pepper, and dried basil. Transfer to another Bowl and maintain warmth.
- Before the pasta is done, heat. One tbsp of olive oil should be added to a large skillet. Quickly sauté sliced garlic cloves for a few minutes on low heat. Stir the arugula and cherry tomatoes for one to two minutes, careful not to let the garlic brown.
- While saving one cup of of the cooking water, drain the pasta. Toss everything together gently and add a splash of the conserved water to lighten the sauce. Add the pasta, pesto, garlic, cherry tomatoes, and arugula directly to the pan. It should not be pasty but saucy, which is how the food should be. Once you get the right consistency, keep adding pasta water. If necessary, add more salt after tasPang. Sliced grilled chicken should be added to the pasta. Garnish with some freshly grated Parmesan or Grano Padano cheese and a few cherry tomatoes for added texture and freshness.

EASY SHRIMP AND ASPARAGUS PASTA

Total Time: 30 Minutes

INGREDIENTS

- 3/4 tsp salt + more to taste and for pasta water
- 1 pound angel hair pasta
- 1 pound peeled and deveined large shrimp (26/30 ct)
- 2 tbsp unsalted butter, divided
- 1 tbsp extra-virgin olive oil
- 1 pound asparagus, trimmed and cut into 2-inch pieces
- 5 cloves garlic, minced
- 2/3 cup of heavy cream*

- Freshly ground pepper to taste
- 1 tsp lemon zest, + wedges for serving
- 1 tsp chopped tarragon (or 1 tbsp parsley)

INSTRUCTIONS

- In a big pot, bring the water to a boil. Use a heaping spoonful of salt.
- To dry the shrimp, pat them with paper towels in the interim.
- Melt one tbsp of butter with oil in a big skillet (not nonstick) over high heat. When the shrimp turn pink and curl, add them in a single layer and fry on one side for one to two minutes. Using tongs, turn the shrimp over and allow it to cook for a full minute or two or Before it is brilliant pink throughout. Toss the shrimp onto a platter.
- In the skillet, melt the last tbsp of butter. When the asparagus begins to soften and the garlic starts to turn brown, add the asparagus and cook, stirring constantly, for one to two minutes.
- Stir and bring the heavy cream to a boil while stirring. After adding 3/4 tsp of salt and pepper, boil the asparagus for about 3 minutes, stirring frequently, Before it becomes crisp-soft.
- Pasta should be added and cooked according to package directions as the water reaches a rolling boil, timing it so the asparagus is already in the pan. Of the pasta cooking liquid, set aside 1 cup of. Make sure to empty well. (If the pasta is done before the shrimp mixture is ready, toss it to avoid sticking together and rinse with water or sprinkle with oil.)
- Incorporate the tarragon and zest from the angel hair lemon, and simmer, tossing and thinning if needed with pasta liquid, Before the pasta is coated with the sauce and the seasoning, asparagus, and shrimp are mixed in. To taste, adjust the seasoning. Along with lemon slices, serve right away.

ZUCCHINI PASTA WITH TOMATOES AND OLIVES

Prep Time: 15 mins | Cook Time: 10 mins | Total Time: 25 mins

INGREDIENTS

- 2–3 Zucchini (spiralized)
- ¼ c Olive Oil
- 2 Garlic Cloves (sliced thin)
- ¼ Cup of Fresh Basil (chopped)
- 2 C Grape Tomatoes (halved/quartered)
- Salt & Pepper to taste
- ¼ Cup of Kalamata Olives (pitted & sliced)
- ¼ Cup of Grated Parm for topping (optional if making vegan)

INSTRUCTIONS

- Zoodles should be spiralized and placed aside.
- In the meantime, warm up some olive oil in a big skillet over medium heat.
- Add the garlic and stir-fry for approximately a minute or Before it turns golden.
- Pour in the grape tomatoes, ½ t pepper, and ½ t salt. Add the basil and olives after lowering the heat to medium-low and stirring for about five minutes or Before the tomato juices clear.
- Take out of the pan and place aside.
- Sauté the "noodles" in the pan Before they become soft.
- Stir in sauce and mix Before well blended. Add additional fresh basil and parmesan cheese on top.

TOMATO RICE

Prep Time: 10 Mins | Cook Time:45 Mins | Total Time: 55mins

INGREDIENTS

- 2 cup ofs of long-grain brown rice
- 2 tbsp olive oil
- 1 yellow onion finely chopped
- 3 garlic cloves minced
- ¼ cup of tomato paste
- 1 tsp cumin
- ½ tsp cinnamon
- 2 Roma tomatoes seeded and finely chopped
- 1 tsp salt
- 3 cup ofs of low-sodium vegetable broth
- ¼ cup of fresh cilantro leaves for garnish

INSTRUCTIONS

- After AddPang the rice in a mesh sieve and rinsing it with cold water Before it is clear, stir it with your hands to release as much starch as possPoundsle. Add aside.
- In a big pot, warm the oil over medium heat. Add onions and simmer for 2 to 3 minutes, stirring now and then, Before softened. Cook the garlic for an additional minute or Before fragrant. After adding the washed rice, tomato paste, cumin, cinnamon, diced tomatoes, and salt, simmer for another two minutes or Before everything is well mixed.
- Once the blend comes to a boil, incorporate the vegetable stock. When the rice is soft and the liquid has been absorbed, reduce heat, cover, and simmer for 45 minutes.
- Take off the heat and let the rice covered to steam for a Another five minutes. Take a fork and uncover and fluff. After serving, top with some fresh cilantro.

LEMONY RISOTTO WITH FRESH HERBS & GARLIC

Prep Time: 15mins | Cook Time: 30mins | Total Time: 45mins

INGREDIENTS

- 3 ½ cup ofs of water
- 1 (14-Ounces.) can light coconut milk
- 1 pinch ground turmeric (optional, for color)
- 2-3 sprigs fresh thyme
- 2 Tbsp vegan butter (we used Miyoko's // or sub olive oil)
- 1 medium shallot, finely diced
- 4 cloves garlic, minced
- 1 tsp lemon zest (~1/2 medium lemon // + more for serving)
- 1 cup of arborio rice
- 1/2 – 3/4 tsp sea salt
- 1/4 cup of dry white wine (such as Sauvignon Blanc or Pinot Gris)
- 2 Tbsp lemon juice
- 1/2 cup of soft herbs of choice (such as parsley, basil, dill, and/or chives // + more for serving)

INSTRUCTIONS

- **Broth:** Heat a medium-sized saucepan with water, coconut milk, and turmeric, if desired. Simmer, stirring, over medium heat. Once the mixture reaches a simmer, turn down the heat to maintain warmth. To give the soup a wonderful herbaceous flavor, add some thyme sprigs!
- **Risotto:** Place a big skillet with a rim over medium heat. After adding the olive oil or vegan butter, shallot, and simmer for three to five minutes, stirring now and again, Before the shallot becomes pretty transparent. Cook after adding the garlic and lemon zest for one minute or Before fragrant.

After lowering the heat to medium-low:

- Add the salt and arborio rice.

- Cook, stirring, for one minute to coat.
- When the liquid is absorbed, boil the dry white wine for one to two minutes while stirring regularly.
- With a spoon or measuring cup of, slowly add 1/2 cup of (120 ml) of the warmed broth at a time, stirring nearly all the while to allow the risotto to reheat gently. A gentle simmer should always be present, and the heat should be medium. The mixture should be heated but not boiling. Otherwise, it will cook too quickly and get sticky.
- Stirring constantly, keep adding broth Before the rice is al dente or cooked through but still somewhat crunchy. The entire process should only take fifteen to twenty minutes (estimate based on original recipe; modify if serving size changes).
- Incorporate the lemon juice and the fresh herbs after the rice is cooked. Taste and modify as necessary, adding extra herbs for flavor and freshness, lemon juice for brightness, or salt for balance.
- When ready to serve, divide the risotto into serving bowls and top with optional additional herbs and lemon zest. Fresh is best, but leftovers can be refrigerated for two to three days with a cover. Reheat in the stovetop or microwave on medium heat, rehydraPang with water or vegetable broth as needed. Not suitable for freezing.

MEDITERRANEAN PAELLA (VEGETARIAN)

Ready In: 42mins

INGREDIENTS

- 2tbsp hot water
- 3 -4Spanish saffron threads
- 2cup ofs of rice (uncooked)
- 1/4cup of extra virgin olive oil
- 4cup ofs of vegetable broth
- 1cup of green beans
- 1cup of black olives (whole)
- 1red bell pepper, chopped
- 1/2 - 1tsp white pepper
- 1/2 - 1tsp cayenne pepper
- 1cup of roma tomato, chopped

DIRECTIONS

- Add two tsp of hot water with the saffron threads in it. Please stir it a little, then Add it aside.
- The raw rice should be sautéed in olive oil for around two minutes in a big pan or Dutch oven while stirring conPanuously.
- Add the bell pepper, green beans, black olives, saffron combination, white pepper, cayenne, tomato, and vegetable broth.
- Cook, covered, Before the water evaporates, stirring now and then to prevent it from adhering to the pot's bottom. Cooking time is 30 minutes.

RIGATONI WITH EGGPLANT, TOMATOES, AND MOUNCESZARELLA

Serves: 4-6

INGREDIENTS

- Olive oil
- 1 pound (448 grams) rigatoni pasta
- 1 small eggplant, diced
- 2 cup ofs of (300 grams) cherry tomatoes, halved
- 1 small onion, chopped
- 1/2 cup of (120mL) white wine
- 1 (28 Ounces or 750 gram can) crushed tomatoes
- 1 (4 Ounces or 112 grams) ball buffalo mOunceszarella, cut into small pieces
- Basil

DIRECTIONS

Warm up a good bit of olive oil in a big skillet over medium heat (be careful; eggplant absorbs a lot of oil). Sauté the eggplant, cherry tomatoes, and onion, tossing frequently Before all the veggies are soft and cooked. If needed, keep adding olive oil as you go. Add salt and pepper to the vegetables to season them. Add the white wine next, and heat for about five minutes, allowing it to evaporate.

After adding the crushed tomatoes:

- Simmer the mixture after bringing the sauce to boil for around ten minutes, stirring occasionally.
- Allow the sauce to conPanue cooking by reducing the heat to a simmer.
- As you wait, prepare the pasta by boiling the water according to the package's instructions.
- Chop some basil, however much you want, and set aside while the noodles and sauce cook.
- ReTransfer the pasta's water.

- When making the Bowl, add salt and pepper to taste the sauce.

Pasta should be added to the sauce along with mOunceszarella and basil. Mix everything and serve immediately, topped with one or two additional basil leaves if desired.

EASY MOROCCAN VEGETABLE TAGINE RECIPE

☐ Total Time: 55 minutes

INGREDIENTS

- ¼ cup of Private Reserve extra virgin olive oil, more for later
- 2 medium yellow onions, peeled and chopped
- 8-10 garlic cloves, peeled and chopped
- 2 large carrots, peeled and chopped
- 2 large russet potatoes, peeled and cubed
- 1 large sweet potato, peeled and cubed
- Salt
- 1 tbsp Harissa spice blend or 1 ½ tsp ras el hanout
- 1 tsp ground coriander
- 1 tsp ground cinnamon
- ½ tsp ground turmeric
- 2 cup ofs of canned whole peeled tomatoes
- ½ cup of heaping chopped dried apricot
- 1 quart low-sodium vegetable broth (or broth of your choice)
- 2 cup ofs of cooked chickpeas
- 1 lemon, juice of
- Handful fresh parsley leaves

INSTRUCTIONS

- Olive oil should be heated to a light shimmer in a big, heavy saucepan or Dutch oven over medium heat. Add onions in and turn the heat up to medium-high. Saute for five minutes, making frequent tosses.
- Include the chopped veggies and garliCup of Add some spices and salt for seasoning. Mix by tossing.
- Stirring frequently with a wooden spoon, cook over medium-high heat for 5 to 7 minutes.
- Add the broth, tomatoes, and apricots. To taste, add a small tsp of salt again.
- Cook for ten minutes with the heat on medium-high. After another 20 to 25 minutes of simmering, the vegetables should be soft and covered at reduced heat.
- After stirring in the chickpeas, Cook for five minutes on low heat.
- Incorporate the lemon juice and fresh parsley and stir. Add extra salt after tasPang and adjusPang the seasoning or your preferred amount of the harissa spice blend.
- After transferring, pour a large amount of Private Reserve extra virgin olive oil over everyserving bowl. Serve hot over rice or couscous or with your favorite bread. Enjoy yourself!

BLACK BEAN STUFFED PEPPERS

Prep Time: 10 Mins | Cook Time: 45 Mins | Total Time: 55 Mins

INGREDIENTS

- 4 Bell Peppers, any color, I used red and green
- 1 TB butter or olive oil
- 1/2 cup of onion, diced
- 2 cloves garlic, minced
- 1 tsp cumin
- 1/2 tsp chili powder
- 1/2 tsp garlic salt
- 1 15 Ounces can black beans, drained and rinsed

- 1/4 cup of cilantro, chopped
- 3/4 cup of salsa
- 1 cup of cooked rice, I used brown rice
- 1 cup of shredded Mexican cheese

INSTRUCTIONS

- Turn the oven on to 350 degrees.
- Take off the peppers' tops, then scrape off the seeds and membranes. Add away.
- Add onions while the butter is melPang in a skillet over medium heat. After about five minutes, cook Before soft. After adding the garlic, heat it for one more minute.
- Add the chili powder, garlic salt, cumin, and black beans and stir. Mash up approximately half of the black beans with the back of a fork. Savour the salsa and cilantro for an additional two minutes. After turning off the heat, mix in the cooked rice.
- After preparing the four peppers, evenly fill them with the black bean and rice mixture and place them inside a baking Bowl. Add a quarter cup of of cheese to everypepper. Place in the oven and bake. Allow the cheese to melt for 30 to 40 minutes or Before the peppers become soft. Enjoy yourself!

SAFFRON RICE WITH MIXED SEAFOOD

Preparation time: 10 min | Cooking time: 16 min

INGREDIENTS

- 2 measuring cup ofs of or 300g long grain rice
- 50 ml 3 tblsp) olive oil
- 1 finely chopped onion
- 400 ml fish stock
- 200g frOuncesen seafood (thawed)
- Saffron
- Salt
- Pepper

PREPARATION

- Run some water over the rice to rinse it.
- Add the rice, diced onion, and olive oil to the bowl. Make a good stir.
- Stir in the defrosted fish.
- Mix in the fish stock and a small amount of saffron.
- Period.
- Close the lid and turn the light on.
- After roughly sixteen minutes of cooking, the appliance automatically Turnes to "keep warm."

MEDITERRANEAN COLD RICE SALAD WITH HERBS AND FETA

Prep Time: 5mins | Cook Time: 45mins | Total Time: 50mins

INGREDIENTS

- 1 cup of brown rice
- 2 cup ofs of water
- 1 tsp kosher salt
- 1/4 cup of extra virgin olive oil
- 1 lemon juiced
- 1 garlic clove minced
- 1 can cannellini beans drained and rinsed
- 2 Tbsp fresh oregano finely chopped
- 2 Tbsp fresh parsley finely chopped
- 1 Tbsp fresh chives minced
- 4 ounces feta cheese crumbled
- Kosher salt and pepper to taste

INSTRUCTIONS

- After bringing water, rice, and a tsp of salt to a boil, cover, lower the heat, and boil Before the rice is soft, about 40 minutes soft, and all liquid has been absorbed. Cover and leave for five minutes. Use a fork to fluff. Let cool to room temperature.
- Mix the herbs, garlic, lemon juice, and olive oil in a bowl. Dredge in cooked and cooled rice. Mix in the feta and beans just till incorporated.
- Adjust seasoning to taste.
- Either room temperature or a cooled serving is OK.

SARAH'S FETA RICE PILAF

Prep Time:10 Mins | Cook Time:40 Mins | Total Time:50 Mins

INGREDIENTS

- 2 tbsp butter
- ½ cup of orzo pasta
- ½ cup of diced onion
- 2 cloves garlic, minced
- 2 cup ofs of chicken broth
- ½ cup of white rice
- 1 cup of chopped spinach
- ½ cup of chopped Bulgarian feta cheese

DIRECTIONS

- Grease a skillet over medium-low heat; add the orzo and cook, stirring, for 3 to 5 minutes or Before golden brown. Add the onion and stir. Cook for 5 to 10 minutes, stirring now and then. After about a minute, stir in the garlic Before fragrant.
- Before boiling, add the rice and stock to the orzo-onion mixture. Simmer the rice for 20 to 25 minutes, or Before it is soft and the liquid has been absorbed while reducing the heat to medium-low and covering the skillet.
- Stir in the feta and spinach after removing from the heat. Cover and leave as the feta melts and the spinach wilts, which should take around five minutes. With a fork, fluff.

TOMATO-BASIL RISOTTO

Prep Time:15 mins | Cook Time:1 hr

EQUIPMENT

- 1 microplane
- 1 high sided sauté pan
- 1 large pot or dutch oven

INGREDIENTS

- 2 large tomatoes globe, heirloom, or beefsteak all work
- 1/4 cup of extra-virgin olive oil
- 1/2 small white onion finely diced
- Diamond Crystal kosher salt
- 1 cup of of risotto rice such as Aborio
- 2/3 cup of of dry unoaked white wine
- 2 tbsp salted butter
- 1 cup of fresh basil leaves
- 4 ounces whole milk ricotta
- Freshly ground black pepper

INSTRUCTIONS

- Using a microplane, cut the tomatoes in half and then grate the insides into a small bowl to create a texture that resembles gazpacho. Throw away the skins and reserve.
- A large saucepan should be placed on one burner and filled with five to six cup ofs of of water. Next to it, Add a high-sided sauté pan and set the burner to medium heat.
- Place the onion in the sauté pan and oil. Add a little salt for seasoning, then cook, stirring now and again, for 5 to 7 minutes or Before the onion is soft. After adding a splash of water, sauté the onion for another four to five minutes or Before it is very soft and almost melts. Without allowing it to burn, the water helps it cook Before it becomes soft.

- Add the rice and toss it quickly to ensure that all the rice is covered with oil and onion. Cook for five minutes or Before the rice turns clear on the sides and makes a somewhat clattering sound when it hits the pan's edges. This indicates that the grain has absorbed some of the oil and that the wine should now be added. Allow the wine to simmer for two to three minutes to cook off the alcohol.
- While waiPang, season your large pot of water with a tbsp of kosher salt and gently simmer.
- Pour a generous amount of water (about 1/3 cup of) into the risotto and stir conPanuously for 20 to 25 minutes or Before the water is completely absorbed. Do the same thing again, but scoop out some tomato purée this time. After every three minutes, keep Turning and stirring Before the risotto thickens, smoothes out, and becomes soft.
- After 20 minutes, check the rice; the cooking process is complete if the grains are soft and have lost their bite. Take your time; it could take up to thirty to thirty-five minutes.
- Once the rice is soft, reTransfer the pan from the hob, but do not turn off the heat on either burner. Stir the butter into the risotto after adding it. After that, stir slowly to allow the heat from the risotto to melt the basil into a creamy consistency. To taste, add salt and pepper for seasoning.
- If you're feeling very cheese-loving, add a dollop of ricotta cheese and black pepper to the top of everybowl.

BROWN RICE TABBOULEH

Prep Time: 20 mins | Total Time: 1 h 10 m

INGREDIENTS

- 1/2 cup of uncooked long grain brown rice
- 1 1/2 cup ofs of vegetable broth
- 2 tbsp olive oil
- 2 tbsp lemon juice
- 1/2 tsp minced garlic
- ½ English cucumber, finely diced
- Roma tomatoes, seeded and diced
- 1/3 cup of finely chopped parsley
- 1/4 cup of finely chopped fresh chives
- 2 tbsp finely chopped fresh mint
- 1/4 tsp everysalt and pepper

DIRECTIONS

After washing, carefully drain the rice. After adding the rice to the broth:

- Heat the mixture Before it boils.
- Turn the heat down to a gentle simmer and cover.
- Sauté for 40 to 45 minutes or Before the liquid is absorbed.
- Take off the heat and leave for five minutes.
- Transfer to a sizable bowl and let cool to room temperature after fluffing with a fork.

Olive oil, lemon juice, and garlic should all be mixd in a mixing Bowl. Add the diced cucumber, tomatoes, parsley, chives, and mint; stir Before well mixd. The rice should now be chilled. Use pepper and salt for seasoning Before it's time to serve, cover and chill.

WILD RICE WITH ARTICHOKES AND OLIVES

Prep Time: 20 mins | Cook Time: 35 mins | Total Time:40 mins

INGREDIENTS

- 1 cup of uncooked wild rice
- 1 cup of vegetable broth
- 3/4 cup ofs of water
- 1 cup of marinated artichokes drained
- 1/2 cup of heat-dried tomatoes marinated or not
- 1/3 cup of kalamata olives
- 1 tbsp olive oil divided
- 1/4 tsp kosher salt
- 1/2 tsp pepper
- 1/2 tsp garlic powder
- Juice of 1 1/2 lemons
- 1/4 cup of fresh parsley + more for serving finely chopped

INSTRUCTIONS

- Mix the wild rice, vegetable broth, and water in a medium-sized saucepan. Once the water is completely absorbed, reduce heat to low, cover, and bring to a boil. For ten more minutes, keep the rice covered.
- Meanwhile, coarsely chop the artichokes and kalamata olives (you may even leave the olives whole if you'd like). Cut the heat-dried tomatoes into small pieces.
- Mix the remaining components with the olive oil when the rice is cooked. Toss gently to mix.
- Top with additional freshly cut parsley and serve.

GLUTEN-FREE FLOURLESS ORANGE ALMOND CAKE

Prep Time: 2hours 15minutes | Cook Time: 1hour | Total Time: 3hours 15mins

INGREDIENTS

- 2 navel oranges
- 6 eggs
- 250 g (1 cup of) caster sugar
- 250 g (2 ½ cup ofs of) almond meal
- 1 tsp baking powder
- 50 g flaked almonds
- 2 tbs icing sugar, optional for sprinkling on top

INSTRUCTIONS

Traditional Approach

- Before AddPang the navel oranges into a big saucepan, wash them and reTransfer their ends (discard the ends).
- Simmer, covered, for 2 hours (adding water as needed), then bring to a boil.
- After taking the oranges out of the water, let them cool entirely so they can be handled easily.
- Bake at 160 degrees Celsius (fan-forced) Before golden brown. Before you set it away, grease a 22-centimeter. Whisk together the eggs and caster sugar baking paper in a large bowl.
- After the oranges have cooled, cut them into pieces and pulse them in a blender.
- Whisk or process Before very smooth, with no lumps remaining. ReTransfer off the table.
- Mix the eggs with the caster sugar in a big bowl Before light and foamy, with a hand-held mixer for about 2 minutes on high speed.
- After adding the orange puree, mix well.
- Mix in the baking powder and almond meal.
- Transfer the mixture to the heated baking pan.
- Before serving, garnish the cake with the flaked almonds.

- Cook in the oven for half an hour or Before a spear poked in the center emerges with a few crumbs Added.
- Let it cool in the pan for at least one night before storing it at room temperature.
- Sprinkle with confectioners' sugar right before serving.

Using a Thermomix

- Before AddPang the navel oranges into a big saucepan, wash them and reTransfer their ends (discard the ends).
- Simmer, covered, for 2 hours (adding water as needed), then bring to a boil.
- After taking the oranges out of the water, let them cool entirely so they can be handled easily.
- Bake at 160 degrees Celsius (fan-forced) Before golden brown. Before you set it away, grease a 22-centimeter. Prepare a springform pan by lining the inside and outside with baking paper.
- Add the cooled oranges into the TM bowl once you've chopped them. Process Before smooth, occasionally scraping down bowl sides, then gradually raising to Speed 7. I am reserving one bowl for later use.
- Get the TM bowl dry and clean. After 30 seconds on Speed 5, add the caster sugar and eggs and conPanue mixing.
- Mix on Speed 5 for 10 seconds when the orange puree is added.
- Turn the mixer to Reverse, Speed 3, and mix in the baking powder and almond meal for 20 seconds.
- Transfer the mixture to the heated baking pan.
- Before serving, garnish the cake with the flaked almonds.
- Cook in the oven for half an hour or Before a spear poked in the center emerges with a few crumbs Added.
- Let it cool in the pan for at least one night before storing it at room temperature.
- Sprinkle with confectioners' sugar right before serving.

ROSEMARY AND OLIVE OIL ICE CREAM

Prep Time: 4 hrs 40 mins | Cook Time:20 mins | Total Time:5 hrs

INGREDIENTS

- 1 ½ cup ofs of whole milk
- ½ cup of white sugar
- ¼ cup of brown sugar
- 2 tbsp light corn syrup
- Pinch of flaky sea salt
- 4 fresh rosemary sprigs
- 5 egg yolks
- 1 ½ cup ofs of heavy cream
- 1/3 cup of extra virgin olive oil

INSTRUCTIONS

- Add the milk, brown sugar, corn syrup, salt, rosemary, and sugars into a medium pot. Cook for 10 minutes, stirring often, over medium heat. You should be able to dissolve the sugar, heat the milk, and smell the rosemary in the mixture.
- In the stand mixer's bowl, add the egg yolks. To make the eggs lighter in color and well mixed, beat them on medium speed with the whisk Addment. Take the milk mixture and strain out the rosemary.
- To temper the yolks:
- Slowly pour a ladleful of heated milk into the mixture while the mixer is on the Stir setPang.
- Transfer the egg, whisking constantly while cooking over medium heat Before the custard thickens to the point where it coats a wooden spoon, which should take approximately 2 to 4 minutes.
- ReTransfer from the heat and transfer to a big basin by straining through a fine-mesh sieve.

- Stir in olive oil and heavy cream before covering and refrigeraPang for at least two hours or all night.
- Follow the manufacturer's directions for your specific model of ice cream maker regarding the freezing process. In a KitchenAid, set the mixer to "stir," add the ingredients, and churn for 20 to 30 minutes or Before the desired consistency is achieved. Transfer the whipped cream to an airtight freezer Container and chill Before firm.

FIG DATE GRAIN AND NUT BARS

Prep Time: 15 Mins | Cook Time: 25 Mins | Total Time: 40 Mins

EQUIPMENT

- 1 Thermomix
- 1 USA Mini Loaf Pan (or equiavlent)

INGREDIENTS

- 70 g boiling water
- 100 g molasses, treacle or golden syrup
- 100 grams dates
- 60 g butter cut into small cubes and allow to soften to room temp
- 150 grams dried figs
- 1 tsp baking soda
- ¾ tsp salt
- 140 grams brown sugar
- 60 g espresso coffee 2 shots* see alternative
- 1 large egg
- 1 tsp vanilla
- ½ tsp baking powder
- 200 grams plain flour
- 50 g grams coarsely chopped walnuts
- 150 g seeds Pepita, Almonds, heatflower etc

INSTRUCTIONS

- Bring the oven temperature to 170 degrees Celsius and turn on the fan. Pull out your little loaf pan. Alternatively, you might try greasing it if the nonstick coaPang isn't perfect.
- Mix the molasses and water in the TM bowl according to weight, then cook at 80°C for 3 minutes on speed 1.5.
- While that's happening, roughly chop the figs and dates to your liking. I chopped them in half to make sure all of the dates and figs were the same size.
- Wait for the TM lights to go green before letPang the mixture cool. Please allow 5 to 10 minutes.
- Add the dates, butter, figs, baking soda, salt, brown sugar, and coffee in a bowl and place it on top of the TM cover while you wait. *refer to guidelines
- After the ingredients in the TM bowl have cooled, add the measured ingredients from the previous step, followed by the egg, vanilla, baking powder, and flour. Mix on reverse speed +2 for 30 seconds.
- After greasing the pan, pour in the batter. Top with nuts and seeds. Press down with a fork to incorporate nuts and seeds into the batter. Roast for 20–25 minutes or Before a toothpick inserted in the center comes clean.

HONEY ALMOND BISCOTTI

Ready In: 1hr 10mins | Ingredients:11

INGREDIENTS

- 2cup ofs of flour
- 3/4cup of sugar
- 3/4cup of unblanched whole almonds (ground fine in a blender or food processor, raw or roasted)
- 3/4tsp baking powder
- 1/2tsp baking soda
- 1/2tsp cinnamon
- 1/4tsp salt (optional)
- 3/4cup of unblanched whole almonds (roasted)
- 1/3cup of honey
- 1/3cup of lukewarm water
- 1/2tsp almond extract (optional) or 1 tsp vanilla (optional)

DIRECTIONS

- Get a baking pan that's 13–15 inches long and coat it with cooking spray, foil, or parchment. Heat oven to 350°F.
- Mix the honey and water Before a solution forms; if using almond or vanilla extract, whisk and add the extracts before setPang aside.
- Stir the dry ingredients (whole and ground almonds included) for about a minute to blend.
- Mix the honey and water, then whisk Before a thick dough forms.
- Cut the dough in half and shape it, or roll it out into two 12-inch-long logs; bake them with plenty of space between them because they will expand. To avoid getPang dough on your fingers, lightly warm them with water. The logs can be more easily shaped.

- They need approximately 30 minutes in the oven at 350°F Before they are solid, darkly brown, and have risen significantly. The logs must be baked for half an hour or roughly thirty minutes.
- Once the logs have cooled for 5 to 10 minutes, use a sharp knife to cut them diagonally at 1/2-inch intervals.
- Season with salt and bake for approximately 15 minutes at 300°F or Before the biscotti are golden and thoroughly dried.
- If baking needs to be extended beyond 15 minutes, flip them over to prevent the bottom side from becoming overly brown.
- Once cooled, transfer to a Pan or other airtight container.
- *Note: I often purchase raw almonds and roast them in my oven at 300°F for 10-15 minutes, stirring after 10 minutes. Leave out of recipes Before cooled to room temperature.

FRESH FRUIT SALAD WITH HONEY LEMON DRESSING

Prep Time:5mins | Chill Time:3hrs | Total Time:3hrs 5mins

INGREDIENTS

- 10-12 cup ofs of assorted fresh berries and fresh fruit blueberries, raspberries, kiwi, melon, strawberries, etc
- 1/3 cup of bottled or fresh lemon juice
- 1/3 cup of honey
- 1 tsp ground cinnamon

INSTRUCTIONS

- Add the fruit in a big basin after washing and slicing it if necessary. Drain it. Mix thoroughly.
- Fresh fruit and berries, 10 to 12 cup ofs of
- Honey, cinnamon, and lemon juice should be thoroughly mixed in a small bowl. Before serving, toss the fruit in the sauce to coat it.
- a quarter cup of of honey and one-third cup of of sugar, either fresh or bottled lemon juice, and one tsp of ground cinnamon

- Stir before serving and let chill for a few hours.

HEALTHY CUTFAST EGG MUFFINS

Total Time: 40 minutes | Yield: 12 egg muffins

INGREDIENTS

- Extra virgin olive oil for brushing
- 1 small red bell pepper, chopped (about ¾ cup of)
- 12 cherry tomatoes, halved
- 1 shallot, finely chopped
- 6 to 10 pitted kalamata olives, chopped
- 3 to 4 Ounces/113 g cooked chicken or turkey, boneless, shredded
- 1 Ounces/ 28. 34 g (about ½ cup of) chopped fresh parsley leaves
- Handful crumbled feta to your liking
- 8 large eggs
- Salt and Pepper
- ½ tsp Spanish paprika
- ¼ tsp ground turmeric (optional)

INSTRUCTIONS

- Before heaPang, center the oven and rack it to 350 degrees Fahrenheit.
- Get a 12-cup of muffin pan (or 12 separate muffin cup ofs of) ready. Add EVOO on the bristles.
- It would help if you filled everyof the 12 cup ofs of up to three-quarters of the way with the vegetables, then add the olives, shallots, peppers, chicken (or turkey), parsley, and crumbled feta.
- Measure out the eggs and mix them with the salt, pepper, and spices in a big bowl or measuring cup of. Mix thoroughly by whisking.
- Cut the egg mixture and fill everycup of halfway, leaving a little gap at the top (approximately three-quarters of the way).

- Set a sheet pan on top of the muffin pan or cup ofs of to avoid messy cleanup. Wait Before the egg muffins have set, which should take around 25 minutes in a heated oven.
- After the muffins have cooled for a few minutes, loosen them by running a Pany butter knife down their edges. Take it out of the pan and enjoy!

APRICOT LAVENDER JAM

Prep Time:20 mins | Cook Time: 25 mins | Total Time: 45 mins

INGREDIENTS

- 3 cup ofs of apricots halved, pitted, and chopped
- 2 sprigs dried lavender flowers approx 1/2 tsp - try 3/4 tsp for bolder flavour
- 1/4 cup of water
- 2 tbsp fresh lemon juice
- 1 1/4 cup ofs of granulated sugar

INSTRUCTIONS

- Toss the apricots, lavender, water, and lemon juice into a medium-sized saucepan and boil, stirring regularly, over medium heat. Simmer, stirring periodically, over low heat for around 5 minutes or Before the fruit wits.
- Cook for 10 to 15 minutes after adding the sugar, or at least Before the fruit is soft and the jam is thick. If foam forms on top, skim it off and throw it away.
- Cut the jam between two half-pint sterile mason Containers. Add a clean cloth to the rims, and then screw the lids on Before they are finger-tight.
- Boil some water and process the Containers. Typically, I accomplish this by quickly boiling water in my largest saucepan Before it reaches a point where it covers the Containers completely. To ensure proper vacuum sealing, place the Containers into the boiling water with the help of tongs or a Container lifter. Allow the lids to 'pop' inwards after 10-15 minutes. When the Containers have cooled enough to handle, you may find that the lids pop.
- Cool the Containers after removing them from the water bath. Unless the middle of the lid dips down, or if it springs back, it has not sealed. First, enjoy the Containers by placing them in the fridge.

- You can keep all the other Containers in a dark, dry area for up to a year.

CAPER CHICKEN CACCIATORE

Servings:5 | Yield:4 servings

INGREDIENTS

- 1 (4 pound) chicken, cut into pieces
- salt and pepper to taste
- ¼ cup of olive oil
- 2 onions, thinly sliced
- ½ cup of fresh sliced mushrooms
- 1 (14.5 ounce) can stewed tomatoes
- 1 (10.75 ounce) can condensed cream of mushroom soup
- 1 cup of white wine
- ¼ cup of pitted green olives
- ¼ cup of black olives
- 2 tbsp capers
- 8 ounces pepperoni sausage, sliced

DIRECTIONS

- Melt the oil in a big skillet over medium heat. Before browning the chicken in high oil, season it with salt & pepper to taste. Lift chicken pieces out of the pan. ReTransfer off the table.
- Lightly brown the mushrooms and onions in the same pan. Add the chicken back in the pan and stir the soup, wine, and tomatoes. Toss in the pepperoni, green and black olives, capers, and simmering liquids. Bring to a simmer over low heat while covered for half an hour.
- Set oven temperature to 350 degrees Fahrenheit or 175 degrees Celsius. After taking the cover off the skillet, Fill a 9-by-13-inch baking Bowl with the mixture.

Heat the oven to a warmed state and bake for approximately 15 minutes, or Before the chicken is cooked and the fluids drain.

GARLIC AND HERB ROAST TURKEY BREAST

Prep time: 30mins | Cook time: – 45 Mins

INGREDIENTS

For Turkey

- 2 ½ lb bone-in turkey breast this would be ½ of a whole turkey breast
- Kosher salt this is the one I use
- 1 tsp/2 g ground allspice
- 1 tsp/2.3 g paprika
- 1 tsp/ 2.3 g ground black pepper
- ½ tsp/ 1.2 g nutmeg
- 1 head garlic about 14 cloves, peeled and minced
- Large handful of chopped fresh parsley about 2 ounces
- Private Reserve extra virgin olive oil
- 7 to 8 small shallots peeled and halved
- 7 celery sticks cut into large pieces

For Grapes

- 1 lb/450 g seedless red grapes
- Private Reserve extra virgin olive oil
- Kosher salt

INSTRUCTIONS

- Add salt to the turkey. Mix the kosher salt into the turkey breast and pat it dry. Season both sides; they also make sure to season inside the skin. Allow it to rest for half an hour at room temperature. However, for optimal results, cover and refrigerate the turkey for at least two hours or perhaps overnight (see notes for more information).

- After chilling the turkey, please reTransfer it from the refrigerator and let it come to room temperature. ReTransfer from heat and set aside while you make the rest of the ingredients.

- Grill the grapes. Get the oven hot, about 450 degrees Fahrenheit. Heat a 9 ½ x 13 baking pan (I use a cast-iron pan similar to this one) and add the grapes. Mix with a pinch of salt and a drizzle of extra-virgin olive oil. After 15 minutes of roasPang in a heated oven, take the grapes out and set them on a plate to cool. Keep the oven turned on.

- Use the Spice Mixture, Garlic, and Fresh Parsley to season the Turkey. Mix the spices in a small bowl. Once again, delicately peel the skin and spread the spice mixture underneath the turkey. Then, season it all over. Mix the parsley, garlic, and around A quarter to half cup of of extra-virgin olive oil in a big basin. Pour the garlic and parsley mixture over the turkey, being sure to get under the skin as well. Place the turkey in the bowl and coat it well.

- Heat a pan and arrange the turkey breast on top. Add the shallots and celery in the same pan you used before to create a bed for the turkey. An olive oil drizzle and kosher salt are all needed for seasoning. Next, lay the turkey breast on its side.

- Sauté the turkey breast Before it is just cooked through. After preheaPang the oven to 450 degrees F, place the turkey pan on the center rack and reduce heat to 350 degrees F. Cook in a heated oven for 45 minutes or Before the internal temperature reaches 150–155 degrees Fahrenheit. Keep an eye on the turkey occasionally; if the skin gets too brown while roasPang, tent it with foil and keep cooking.

- Return Grapes to the Mix. Carefully take the turkey out of the oven as you near the conclusion of the roasPang time and sprinkle on the grapes. Warm the grapes in the oven for a minute or two; if your turkey wants a little color, broil it for a few minutes as you monitor it closely.

- Take it out of the oven and let it rest quickly before you serve it. Drape some foil over the turkey and set it aside to rest for approximately 15 minutes before carving to serve. The turkey's internal temperature has to be at least 165 degrees Fahrenheit as it conPanues to cook.

- Slice or Carve the Breast of the Turkey. Transfer the breast of the turkey to a sterile chopping board. Carve your way down from the breast bone, keeping your knife near the rPoundss the whole while. After deboning the breast, cut it crosswise into pieces.

CHICKEN STUFFED WITH SPINACH, FETA, AND PINE NUTS

Total:40 mins | Yield:4 servings

INGREDIENTS

- 5 ounces fresh spinach, chopped
- ½ cup of (2 ounces) crumbled feta cheese
- 2 tbsp pine nuts, toasted
- 1 tsp fresh thyme, minced
- 2 tsp fresh lemon juice
- 2 garlic cloves, minced
- 4 (6-ounce) skinless, boneless chicken breast halves
- ¼ tsp salt
- ¼ tsp freshly ground black pepper
- 1 tbsp olive oil
- ½ cup of fat-free, lower-sodium chicken broth

INSTRUCTIONS

- Turn the oven on high heat (350 degrees).
- Place a big ovenproof skillet that is nonstick in a medium-high heat pan. Toss in the spinach and heat, stirring constantly, to wilt the spinach, which should take about a minute. Press the spinach in a colander Before it is just slightly damp. Clean the pan.
- Stir together the spinach, cheese, almonds, thyme, lemon juice, and garliCup of To make a pocket, cut a horizontal slit across the thickest part of everychicken breast half. Add three tsp of filling into everypocket. Use wooden picks to seal. Add salt and pepper to the chicken.

- Add oil to a pan and heat it over medium-high heat. Before adding the chicken, brown it on all sides for about 3 minutes. Saute the broth with the lid on. Add the pan to the oven. ConPanue baking for another 15 minutes at 350°.

MEDITERRANEAN HERB CRUSTED BEEF SOFTLOIN

Prep Time: 15 Minutes | Cook Time: 30 Minutes | Additional Time: 1 Hour | Total Time: 1 Hour 45 Minutes

INGREDIENTS

- 1 ¾ lb. beef softloin
- 4 garlic cloves, minced
- ½ cup of chopped fresh parsley
- 6 tbsp chopped fresh oregano
- 3 tbsp chopped fresh rosemary
- 2 tbsp chopped fresh thyme
- 1 lemon, zested
- 6 tbsp extra virgin olive oil
- 2 tbsp lemon juice, freshly squeezed
- 2 tsp kosher salt
- 1 tsp black pepper
- ½ tsp red pepper flakes

INSTRUCTIONS

- Bring Out the Rub
- Separate the herbs by chopping them. After you mince the garlic, leave it aside.
- Mix the garlic and herbs in a big basin. Before adding the lemon juice, olive oil, and salt, season with salt, pepper, and red pepper flakes in the casserole Bowl, and zest the lemon right into it. Mix the rub thoroughly using a spoon.
- ReTransfer off the table.
- Get the Meat Ready

- Be sure to trim the beef softloin of any excess fat or silver skin if it hasn't been done before. (Since it saves me time, I always have the butcher take care of this.)
- Set the meat softloin aside. To make sure the meat cooks evenly, tuck down the end that is thinner than the other to make it the same thickness. (Your butcher can add his expertise to this, too.)
- Coat the meat well with the rub created using your hands. It should be covered completely. There will be a lot of friction.
- Place the Bowl and beef in the fridge for 30 to 45 minutes.
- Sear the Meat
- Arrange the oven rack to the 425°F position.
- Arrange the beef softloin on a metal baking pan after it has cooled. For easy internal temperature monitoring while roasPang, insert a metal thermometer into the middle of one end of the softloin. (Just so it's known, this is helpful.)
- After 30 minutes in the oven, reTransfer from the oven. Take the meat out of the oven when the thermometer registers 130 degrees Fahrenheit. (My old oven thought it would take 39 minutes.)
- Allow the meat to rest for at least fifteen to twenty minutes. After taking the meat out of the oven, it will keep cooking. We aim for an ideal medium rare for an interior temperature of 135°F.
- Slice the meat and serve it warm once it has rested for the recommended duration.

CATALAN-STYLE RABBIT STEW WITH SHERRY, MUSHROOMS, AND ALMONDS

Cook:3 Hours 30 Minutes

INGREDIENTS

- Kosher salt
- ½ cup of olive oil, divided
- 1 whole rabbit (2½–3 lb.), cut into 11 pieces (see headnote)
- 7 Ounces. coarsely chopped mushrooms (preferably a variety; about 2¼ cup ofs of
- 2 garlic cloves, coarsely chopped
- 1 medium green bell pepper, finely chopped
- 1 medium onion, finely chopped
- ⅓ cup of raw blanched almonds, finely ground in a food processor or mortar and pestle
- 1 cup of dry sherry
- Kosher salt and freshly ground black pepper

INSTRUCTIONS

- After patPang it dry using paper towels, lPoundserally sprinkle salt over the rabbit. Add 1/4 cup of to a big saucepan over medium-high heat for the oil. After it's hot and shimmering, throw in the rabbit and sear it for approximately 8 minutes, flipping once, Before it's brown all over. Please Add it on a plate after transferring it with tongs.
- Turn the heat to medium and add the garlic, mushrooms, and two tbsp of oil to the saucepan. After around five to seven minutes of cooking, toss the mushrooms occasionally to prevent them from sticking. Place on top of the rabbit's plate.
- Place the remaining oil, bell pepper, and onion in the saucepan. Approximately 10 minutes of cooking time is required, tossing frequently Before the veggies are soft and transparent. After reserving the mushrooms and rabbit, add the almonds and sherry and mix well. Add salt to taste. Reduce the sherry by two-thirds over medium heat for around seven or eight minutes. Cover and reduce

heat to low once you've added 2 cup ofs of of water, just enough to cover the rabbit. For 2½-3 hours, or Before the rabbit reaches softness, stir occasionally while cooking.

ITALIAN BRAISED CHICKEN WITH TOMATOES AND OLIVES

Prep: 20 mins | Cook: 40 mins | Total: 1 hr

INGREDIENTS

- 8 bone-in chicken thighs (skin on or off, your choice)
- ½ tsp EACH: salt and pepper
- 2 tbsp olive oil
- 1 medium onion (finely minced)
- 4 cloves garlic (chopped)
- 4 tbsp tomato paste
- 28 ounce can diced tomatoes
- 1 cup of coarsely chopped olives
- 2 tbsp EACH: capers and balsamic vinegar
- 1 tsp EACH: chopped rosemary and oregano
- 1 pinch red pepper flakes
- 1 tsp honey

INSTRUCTIONS

- The oven temperature should be set to 400 degrees Fahrenheit. Rub some salt and pepper onto the chicken.
- Quarter tsp of salt and pepper for everyof eight bone-in chicken thighs
- In a big, ovenproof skillet, heat the oil Before it shimmers. The chicken thighs should be cooked in a pan, and the skin should be sided up for three to four minutes. Cook for another 5 to 6 minutes or Before the other side of the chicken is browned and crispy. Take the chicken out of the pan. (Prepare the remaining ingredients as the chicken cooks.)

- 2 tbsp canola oil
- Reserve approximately two tbsp of the cooking oil and pour it out of the pan. Sauté the onion for three or four minutes or Before it becomes soft. Saute the garlic for a Another minute. When the tomato paste has gotten slightly darker and begun to smell fragrant, reTransfer it from the heat about 3 minutes after adding it to the pan.
- Four cloves of garlic, one medium onion, and four tbsp of tomato paste
- Before adding anything else to the pan, mix everything thoroughly. Garnish with black pepper and sea salt on top. Skin side up, place the chicken breasts back into the skillet. Cook the chicken for 40 minutes in the oven. Serve the chicken immediately after taking it out of the oven.
- 1/2 tsp of balsamic vinegar, two tbsp of minced oregano and rosemary, one pinch of red pepper flakes, one tsp of honey, 28 ounces of diced tomatoes, 1 cup of of roughly chopped olives, two tbsp of capers, and one tsp of lemon juice

LAMB SOUVLAKI WITH TZATZIKI

Prep Time:20 minutes | Cook Time:10 minutes | MarinaPang Time:4 hours | Total Time: 4hours30minutes

EQUIPMENT

- Griddle pan
- Mixing bowls
- 8 Skewers

INGREDIENTS

For the lamb souvlaki

- 1 ½ lb boneless lamb leg or shoulder, cut into 1 ½ inch cubes
- 1 ½ tsp dried oregano
- ¾ tsp cumin
- ¾ tsp paprika
- 1 ½ tsp kosher salt
- ¾ tsp freshly ground black pepper

- 4 tbsp extra virgin olive oil
- 3 cloves garlic, peeled and bashed

For the tzatziki

- ¼ cucumber, grated and squeezed dry in kitchen paper, ½ cup of after squeezing.
- 1 cup of Greek yoghurt, 250 g
- 1 small of garlic clove, finely grated, or half a normal clove
- 1 tbsp red wine vinegar
- 1 tbsp extra virgin olive oil
- ½ tsp kosher salt
- ⅛ tsp freshly ground black pepper

To serve (optional)

- Greek salad
- fries, seasoned with oregano salt
- pita
- orzo rice
- tzatziki
- Instructions

INSTRUCTIONS

- The tzatziki shall be
- Use a mango knife to slice the cucumber coarse grater thinly. Roll up the grated cucumber in two layers of waxed paper. Get the cucumber completely dry by squeezing it.
- A quarter of a cucumber
- To make the cucumber salad, mix the cucumber with Greek yogurt, garlic, and a little. With the olive oil, vinegar made with red wine, salt, and pepper in a basin. If you want to change the seasoning, give it a taste.
- Ingredients: half a cucumber, a cup of of Greek yogurt, a clove of garlic, red wine vinegar, extra virgin olive oil, ½ tsp of kosher salt, and ⅛ tsp of freshly ground black pepper
- As for the souvlaki made with lamb

- Toss the chopped garlic cloves with paprika, olive oil, lamb cubes, cumin, oregano, kosher salt, and black pepper in a big bowl or resealable bag. Coat the lamb thoroughly by mixing it well—Marinate in the refrigerator for at least four hours, preferably all night.
- Three cloves of garlic, four tbsp of extra-virgin olive oil, 1/4 tsp of freshly crushed black pepper, 1 and 3/4 pounds of boneless lamb leg or shoulder, 50% dried oregano, 25% fresh basil, and 25% cumin, 1/4 tsp of paprika, and 1 and 3/4 tsp of kosher salt.
- Boil some water and soak the skewers while the lamb marinates. If desired, thread the lamb cubes and garlic cloves onto skewers.
- For 10 minutes, bring the grill up to 200°C (400°F). Use lightly oiled kitchen paper to brush the grates. Turn the lamb over when it develops excellent grill marks; cook for 4 minutes with the lid closed. ConPanue cooking for 4 minutes before inserPang a probe to test the internal temperature. On the other hand, 145°F is the temperature we prefer. They will get dry if cooked for any longer than that. Tend to it for five minutes after taking it off the heat.
- If desired, the cooked lamb can be accompanied by a warm pita, tzatziki, rice, and fries.
- Tapas, pita, orzo, salad, and tzatziki

VEAL MILANESE (ITALIAN BREADED VEAL CUTLETS)

Prep Time: 15mins | Cook Time: 15mins

INGREDIENTS

- 1 lb Veal cutlets
- 1 cup of Flour
- 2 Eggs
- 1 cup of Breadcrumbs
- Salt & Pepper
- 1/2 cup of Clarified Butter or Cooking Oil for frying
- 1/2 Lemon Quartered

INSTRUCTIONS

- Prepare your Bowles for breading: place flour and bread crumbs on two plates, then beat your eggs in a shallow bowl.
- Add salt and pepper to your veal cutlets for seasoning.
- Bread all the cutlets by sifPang off extra flour, adding the egg, then the breadcrumbs, and AddPang them aside.
- To keep your cooked veal cutlets warm Before you are done frying, heat your oven to a very low 200.
- Heat your cast-iron skillet to around 375 degrees Fahrenheit, then add the clarified butter or oil.
- Fry the veal cutlets in batches on everyside for 3–4 minutes; avoid packing the pan too full, as this will cause the oil to cool down and the cutlets to become mushy.
- Please reTransfer the cooked cutlets and transfer them to a baking sheet-lined rack in the oven to maintain their warmth.
- After the veal cutlets have been fried, arrange them with lemon wedges on a platter and serve.

RICOTTA DIP WITH HERBS & OLIVE OIL

Yield: 6 | Prep Time: 5 Minutes | Total Time: 5 Minutes

INGREDIENTS

- 2 cup ofs of ricotta cheese
- 1 clove garlic
- 2 tbsp extra virgin olive oil + more to drizzle over dip when served
- 1 tsp coarse salt
- 1/2 tsp white pepper
- 1/2 lemon (zest of) and 1 tbsp of the juice
- 1 bunch fresh herbs (such as oregano, thyme, basil, dill, chives, garlic chives, mint etCup of) or 1 heaping tbsp dried herbs (Italian mix or Herbs de Provence)
- 1-2 cured anchovy fillet (optional)*
- 1-2 preserved lemon rinds, thin strip(s) (optional)

INSTRUCTIONS

- Chop the fresh herbs finely and mince the garliCup of With a pestle & mortar or a little fork, pound the preserved lemon rind and anchovies into a paste.
- Transfer the ricotta cheese to a mixing bowl and incorporate the remaining ingredients. Taste and blend to determine flavor. Before serving, Transfer the mixture to a serving Bowl, taste, and adjust the seasoning, olive oil, and herbs. Drizzle with a bit of olive oil.

MEDITERRANEAN SALSA VERDE

Total Time: 13 Mins

INGREDIENTS

- 1 cup of Italian parsley leaves, tightly packed and cleaned (watch our video on how to chop parsley)
- 1-2 medium-sized garlic cloves (green germ or shoot reTransferd)
- 2-3 anchovy filets (substitute with 1 tsp. of anchovy paste in a bowle)
- 1 ½ Tbsp. capers (rinse under water to reTransfer some of the salty brine)
- ½ cup of extra virgin olive oil
- 1 Tbsp. red wine vinegar
- 1 Tbsp. heatdried tomatoes in oil (optional)
- 4-5 mint leaves (optional)
- Salt and fresh ground pepper as need

INSTRUCTIONS

- Grind the garlic, capers, anchovies, and heat-dried tomatoes into a paste in a food processor. You should add a few Tbsp of olive oil to get the components to create a paste.
- Run the red wine vinegar, parsley, and mint leaves in a food processor. Pour olive oil into the machine and process Before pureed. Use more or less salt and pepper as needed to suit your taste. Don't add too much oil; the consistency should be like a pesto.
- Pair with your preferred seafood, meat, or vegetables.

HEAT-DRIED TOMATO PESTO

Prep Time: 5 Mins | Cook Time: 8 Mins | Total Time: 13 Mins

INGREDIENTS

- 1/2 cup of walnuts (or other nut)
- 1 cup of (8 ounces) heat-dried tomatoes packed in oil
- 3 cloves garlic, sliced
- 3/4 cup of grated Parmesan cheese
- 1/2 tsp kosher salt
- 1/4 tsp pepper
- 1/4 tsp chili flakes (optional)
- 1 to 2 roasted red pepper quarters, from a Container (about 1/4 cup of, optional)
- 1/2 cup of extra virgin olive oil

METHOD

- For toast, heat the oven to 350°F the walnuts. Spread the almonds out in a single layer on a sheet pan—toast for 6 to 8 minutes or Before just beginning to become golden and aromatiCup of After taking it out of the oven, let it cool.
- Begin pulverizing the ingredients:
- Add half the heat-dried tomatoes, all the walnuts, cheeses, garlic, chili flakes, salt, pepper, and preserved roasted red pepper (if using) in a food processor or blender. Once properly chopped, pulse a few times.
- Add the remaining tomatoes and oil.
- Add the remaining heat-dried tomatoes and their packed oil after that. (The tomatoes' varied textures will come from CutPang them up.)
- While the engine is operaPang, slowly add the olive oil while scraping down the sides once or twice Before the pesto has a consistent, slightly chunky consistency. (To get a beautiful, toothsome texture, make sure there's still a little chunkiness.)
- Use immediately freeze for up to three months, or keep refrigerated in an airtight Container for up to a week, depending on when you need it.

AIOLI (GARLIC AIOLI)

Prep Time: – 5 Mins | Cook Time:– 5 Mins | Total Time: – 10mins

INGREDIENTS

- 2 cloves garlic, peeled
- ¼ tsp kosher salt
- 1 egg yolk
- ½ cup of extra-virgin olive oil
- 1 tsp fresh lemon juice

INSTRUCTIONS

Prepare: Kitchen towels should be dampened and then wrung out. On the counter, roll the towel into a ring and place a medium bowl in the center. Transfer the oil into a spout-equipped measuring cup of and reserve.

To season the egg yolk:

- Finely shred the garlic into the bowl utilizing a microplane or the little side of a microplane or box grater.
- Add the egg yolk and kosher salt.
- Mix for a short while with a whisk.

Pour in the oil: Slowly whisk in a few drops of oil at a time. When the aioli begins to emulsify, gradually add more oil in a narrow stream while keeping up a rapid whisking tempo.

To ensure that all of the oil has been added and the mixture is fully emulsified:

- Whisk the aioli a few more times.
- Add lemon juice and whisk.
- Taste for salt and make necessary adjustments.

LEMON DILL YOGURT SAUCE

Prep Time:5 mins | Total Time:5 mins

INGREDIENTS

- 1 cup of plain Greek yogurt, I've used anywhere from 2% milk fat to 11% milk fat (just not fat-free)
- 1 to 2 cloves garlic, finely minced (start with 1 clove and see how you like it)
- 1 tbsp lemon zest, optional
- 1 tbsp lemon juice, use a little more to taste if you want more lemon flavour
- 1 tsp dried dill weed, or 3 tsp (1 tbsp) chopped fresh dill
- ½ tsp salt, or to taste
- ½ tsp freshly ground black pepper, or to taste

INSTRUCTIONS

Place the Greek yogurt in a medium-sized mixing basin with yogurt, garlic, lemon zest (if using), lemon juice, dill, salt, and black pepper. Whisk to mix. Add lemon juice, dill, salt, and black pepper to taste the desired seasoning. Serve immediately or keep chilled for up to three or four days in an airtight container. Before serving, give it one more stir.

BRUSCHETTA-STYLE PITA PIZZAS

Yield: 4 Pizzas | Prep Time: 5 Minutes | Cook Time: 10 Minutes | Total Time: 15 Minutes

INGREDIENTS

FOR SAUCE

- 1 small can chopped tomatoes
- 2 cloves garlic
- 2 tsp olive oil
- 1 tsp sugar
- Garlic powder, to taste
- Cayenne pepper, to taste
- 4 whole wheat pita shells
- 1 small container fresh mOunceszarella cheese

INSTRUCTIONS

- To prepare pizza sauce à la bruschetta, Fill a mixing Bowl with an empty can of tomatoes. Garlic should be grated into the tomatoes using a microplane grater. To taste, add sugar, olive oil, and spices. Add aside.
- Set oven temperature to 400 degrees Fahrenheit. To slightly crisp, place the pita shells directly on the oven grate and heat for two to three minutes. Take out of the oven and cover the pita shells with cheese. Return the oven to baking after five more minutes or after the cheese has somewhat melted. ReTransfer the oven again, then top everypizza with a few tbsp of tomatoes. Try to get tomato bits on the crust rather than slathering it in liquid. Add the pizzas back in the oven for one or two more minutes to allow the tomatoes to reheat slightly. Take out of the oven and proceed to serve.

TOMATO BASIL BRUSCHETTA

Prep Time: 31 minutes | Cook Time: 9 minutes | Total Time: 40 minutes

INGREDIENTS

- 2 pounds ripe tomatoes (about 5 to 6 medium tomatoes, but any variety will work)
- ½ tsp fine sea salt, + more to taste
- ½ cup of finely chopped white onion (about ½ medium)
- ½ cup of chopped fresh basil (about ¾ ounce)
- 2 cloves garlic, pressed or minced
- 1 baguette (French bread)
- 4 to 5 tbsp extra-virgin olive oil, divided
- Thick balsamic vinegar (see notes within post) and optional Maldon flaky sea salt

INSTRUCTIONS

- Heat the oven (or a gas grill, if using one) to 450 degrees F. If wanted, quickly clean up by lining a big, rimmed baking sheet with parchment paper. Should your baking sheet be smaller than mine, you should prepare the toast in two batches.
- Chop the tomatoes, leaving the liquid and seeds on the chopping board, and add the diced tomatoes to a medium-sized mixing bowl. When the tomatoes are ripe, add the onion, garlic, and basil and stir to coat them with salt. As you conPanue to work on the bread, stir everything together and leave aside to marinade.
- Cut your baguette into less expansive pieces than ½ inch diagonally (see photographs). My large baking sheet usually holds 20 to 24 pieces so that you may have some leftover bread. Spread a small amount of olive oil over everyside of the slice (two to three tbsp of oil will be needed for this).
- Place everyslice in a single layer on the baking sheet that has been prepared, and bake them for 6 to 9 minutes on the middle rack or Before the tops are crisp and attractively golden. Transfer the toasts to a serving tray or platters and set them aside if preferred.

- Using your palm as a stopgap, carefully drain any extra tomato liquid gathered in the bowl when ready to serve. Pour in the final two tbsp of olive oil. After stirring it, add more salt to taste (I usually add another ¼ to ½ tsp). Add another squeezed clove of garlic if you don't think your bruschetta has enough garlic flavor (I like mine cooked just enough).
- Spread the tomato mixture over everytoast, pressing your spoon against the bowl to squeeze off any extra juice. Drizzle a few tsp of thick balsamic vinegar over the top, and if you have any flaky salt, sprinkle it over very lightly. It is better to serve bruschetta right away.

MEDITERRANEAN VEGGIE PIZZA

Prep Time:30minutes | Cook Time:20minutes | Total Time:50minutes

INGREDIENTS

- 1 envelope Fleischmann's® RapidRise Yeast
- 2- 2 ½ cup of flour
- 1 ½ tsp sugar
- ¾ tsp salt
- ⅔ cup of very warm water
- 6 tbsp oil, divided
- ½ tsp dried thyme
- ¼ tsp dried oregano
- ¼ tsp dried parsley
- ½ cup of chopped artichoke hearts
- ⅓ cup of heat dried tomatoes packed in oil, drained
- ⅓ cup of kalamata olives, sliced
- ¼ red onion, thinly sliced
- ¼ cup of crumbled feta cheese
- optional toppings: fresh basil, cracked black pepper, coarse sea salt

- Set the oven's temperature to 425.
- Add the yeast, sugar, salt, and one cup of of flour to a sizable basin. Stir in 3 tbsp oil and water, and mix Before thoroughly mixd about 1 minute. Add enough of the remaining flour gradually to form a soft dough. The dough will be sticky and should be shaped into a ball.
- Using a floured surface, knead by hand for approximately 4 minutes, adding more flour Before the dough is smooth and elastiCup of At this time, give the dough ten minutes to rest.
- Roll out your dough Before it is about 1/4 inch, then place it on a baking sheet that has been lightly oiled. Add three tbsp of olive oil and scatter some dried herbs on top. Add olives, heat-dried tomatoes, onions, and artichokes on top.
- The dough should be cooked through after about 15 minutes of baking on the lowest rack. I like to BAKE for the first 12 minutes to obtain a well-browned crust and then Turn to BROIL for the final 2-3 minutes. Garnish with feta cheese, salt, pepper, and fresh basil (keep an eye on it to prevent burning). Serve right away.

WHOLE WHEAT MARGHERITA PIZZA

Prep time:20 mins | Cook time:30 mins | Total time:50 mins

INGREDIENTS

- 1 recipe Pizza dough
- 1.25 cup of Homemade Marinara sauce
- 1 ball of MOunceszarella cheese (340 grams)
- 2-3 small Tomatoes, cut in circles
- 1/4 cup of Roughly teared up Basil leaves
- 2-3 tbsp Olive oil to brush the base

INSTRUCTIONS

- Set oven temperature to 350°F. Add the pizza ingredients together.
- Homemade sauce for marinara. Click the page above to create marinara sauce at home; however, any store-bought pizza sauce will do.
- To prepare your homemade pizza dough, click the website above.
- Before adding the sauce, I want my foundation to be toasted. I thus topped the base with beans and cooked it for eight to ten minutes at 350 degrees Fahrenheit.
- After removing the beans, preserve them for later use. For a crispier crust, I like to spray. Add olive oil to the pizza's base and borders before adding sauce and toppings.
- It's time to cover the bottom with marinara sauce.
- Add slices of tomato on top.
- Add the basil leaves and mOunceszarella cheese generously.
- Although the marinara sauce already contains salt, you can now season your pizza if you'd like.
- Place the pizza in a heated oven.
- Bake Before the cheese is golden, 15 to 20 minutes, starts to bubble and caramelize in the center, and the crust is golden brown. The cooking time may change depending on your oven.
- Pizza should be taken out of the oven and left on the counter for a few minutes to soften the cheese and vegetables. Slice it, top with red chili flakes, and dig in!

- Pizza bases can be prepared ahead of time. Bake them with sauce, cheese, and your preferred toppings when ready.

ZA'ATAR PITA WITH GARLIC LABNEH

Total: 1 day (includes draining, rising and cooling times) | Active: 35 min

INGREDIENTS

Labneh:

- 3 cup ofs of (750 milliliters) full fat plain yogurt
- 1 garlic clove, finely minced
- 3/4 tsp kosher salt

Pita:

- 1 1/2 cup ofs of (210 grams) bread flour, + more if needed
- 1/2 cup of (65 grams) whole wheat flour
- 2 tsp (10 grams) sugar
- 1 tsp instant yeast
- 1/2 tsp kosher salt
- 3/4 cup of (180 milliliters) warm water
- 1 tbsp (15 milliliters) olive oil, + more for the bowl

Za'atar/Garnish:

- 1 tbsp ground cumin
- 1 tbsp dried oregano
- 1 tbsp sesame seeds
- 1 tbsp sumac
- 2 tsp dried thyme
- 1 tsp dried marjoram (or extra oregano)
- 1 tsp kosher salt
- 1/2 tsp ground coriander
- 1/2 tsp freshly ground black pepper or crushed red peppe

Fresh mint:

- Extra-virgin olive oil
- Fresh or quick pickled cucumber, tomatoes, turnip, and/or onions
- Olives

DIRECTIONS

To make the labneh:

- Cover a bowl with a fine-mesh cheesecloth or a couple of layers of sieve lined with a clean kitchen towel.
- Transfer the yogurt mixture to the sieve with lining after mixing it with the garlic and salt.
- After covering the yogurt with the folded towel or cheesecloth, add a heavy can on top.
- Add the mixture in the refrigerator to drain for at least 24 to 48 hours or Before it thickens and becomes spreadable.
- After the whey has drained, discard any leftovers and store them in the refrigerator for up to three weeks in a sealed container.

To make the pita, mix the kosher salt, sugar, quick yeast, bread flour, and whole wheat flour in a sizable bowl or a stand mixer bowl. Fill a well in the center with olive oil and warm water. To make a shaggy dough, mix. After 3 to 4 minutes of kneading the dough, add additional flour if necessary. Transfer the dough to a basin that has been lightly oiled, cover it with a dinner plate, and place it in a warm location to rise for one and a half hours. Or Before it has doubled in size.

In the meantime, prepare the za'atar by AddPang the cumin, coriander, crushed red pepper, sumac, thyme, marjoram, and sesame seeds in a small container. Could you give it a good shake to blend?

Punch down the dough, take it out of the bowl, Add it on a surface that has been lightly floured, and shape it into six equal balls. Place everypiece on a large baking sheet covered with parchment paper and roll it into an oval or round shape 1/4 to 1/2 inch thick. Add a sprinkling of za'atar to everyand gently press to cling. Place the Bowl warmly for 20 to 30 minutes, or Before it rises slightly, and cover with a fresh kitchen towel.

In the interim, set your oven to 500 degrees Fahrenheit (260 degrees Celsius).

Bake for 5 to 6 minutes or Before the pitas are puffy but not browned. Transfer the pita on a cooling rack made of wire.

To present, transfer the labneh into a serving Bowl and top it with extra virgin olive oil, fresh mint, and additional za'atar. Accompany with pita, some pickled or fresh veggies, and a few olives.

BEEF GYROS WITH TZATZIKI SAUCE

Prep Time:30 mins | Additional Time:45 mins | Total Time:1 hr 15 mins

INGREDIENTS

- Tzatziki Sauce
- 1/2 of a 6-ounce carton plain fat-free Greek yogurt
- ½ cup of shredded, seeded cucumber
- 1 ½ tsp red wine vinegar
- 1 ½ tsp snipped fresh dill
- 1 clove garlic, minced
- ¼ tsp kosher salt
- Beef Gyros
- Nonstick cooking spray
- 1 cup of chopped onion
- 2 tbsp water
- 1 pound lean ground beef (95% lean)
- 1 egg
- ¼ cup of dry whole-wheat bread crumbs
- 4 tsp dried oregano, crushed
- 2 tsp dried marjoram, crushed
- 3 cloves garlic, minced
- ½ tsp kosher salt
- ½ tsp black pepper
- 8 low-carb pita bread rounds

- 3 medium roma tomatoes, sliced
- ½ cup of thinly sliced cucumber
- ¼ cup of thinly sliced red onion
- ½ cup of crumbled reduced-fat feta cheese (2 ounces)

DIRECTIONS

- To make Tzatziki Sauce, mix Greek yogurt, cucumber, red wine vinegar, dill, minced garlic, and salt in a small bowl when it's time to serve, cover and refrigerate for up to four hours.
- Get the beef gyros ready: Set oven temperature to 325°F. Grease a 9 x 5-inch loaf pan with cooking spray and place parchment paper within.
- Add one cup of of onion and the water in a food processor, cover it, and process Before it is smooth. To eliminate extra liquid, strain the pureed onion through a fine-mesh strainer and dispose of the liquid. Add the onion back in the food processor. Add the egg, bread crumbs, garlic, oregano, marjoram, salt and pepper, and ground meat. Process the mixture with a cover on Before a paste forms.
- After filling a loaf pan with the meat mixture, press it lightly. Grease a 13 x 9-inch baking sheet in the loaf pan. The baking pan should be filled with enough boiling water to reveryhalfway up the loaf pan's edges. Bake (see Tip) for 35 to 40 minutes or Before done (160 degrees F). ReTransfer any fat. Let cool for ten minutes. After removing, cut into 1/4-inch-thick slices.
- Place slices of meat, tomato, cucumber, and red onion inside the pita bread, then cover with cheese. Add Tzatziki Sauce to the Bowl.

SAUSAGE AND WHITE BEAN BRUSCHETTA

Total Time: 20 Min

INGREDIENTS

- 1 lb Italian sausage, casings reTransferd
- 2 14.5-Ounces cans fire roasted diced tomatoes
- 6 Ounces fresh spinach*
- 14.5-Ounces can white beans, drained
- To serve: Garlic toast (see recipe notes), grated parmesan, balsamic vin or glaze

DIRECTIONS

- Sausage should be browned in a skillet over medium heat and crumbled with a wooden spoon. Simmer after adding the tomatoes. Stir in the spinach and simmer for a few more or two minutes Before the spinach has wilted (if using frOuncesen spinach, this could take up to an additional minute or two).
- Add white beans and season with salt and pepper to taste. It's done when the white beans are just heated through.
- Garlic toast should be topped with sausage and white beans, then drizzled with balsamic glaze or vinegar and grated parmesan cheese.

GRILLED VEGGIE AND HUMMUS PITAS

Prep Time:15 mins | Cook Time:15 mins | Total Time: 30 mins

INGREDIENTS

- 1 zucchini
- 1 squash
- 2 to matoes
- ½ small yellow onion
- ½ pound bella mushrooms
- ⅛ cup of balsamic vinegar or glaze Trader Joe's has an excellent one
- ½ cup of olive oil divided
- ⅓ cup of parmesan cheese divided
- salt
- pepper
- 3 pita pockets
- Hummus

INSTRUCTIONS

To prevent your vegetables from falling off the skewers before grilling:

- Chop them up into large chunks.
- Marinate everyvegetable in olive oil, parmesan, salt, and pepper, except for the mushrooms.
- Marinate mushrooms in glaze or balsamic vinegar.

Set your grill to 350 degrees. For uniform cooking times, arrange similar vegetables on the same skewer. Vegetables should be grilled Before soft and slightly browned on the edges. ReTransfer the skewers gently onto a platter.

Halve the pitas and cover with a slightly moist paper towel—microwave for 30 to 1 minute or Before heated through.

Place hummus inside heated pitas and garnish with grilled vegetables.

ROASTED CHICKEN PROVENÇAL

Total Time: 1 hour 15 minutes

INGREDIENTS

- 4chicken legs or 8 bone-in, skin-on chicken thighs
- 2tsp kosher salt
- 1tsp freshly ground black pepper
- ½ to ¾cup of all-purpose flour
- 3tbsp olive oil
- 2tbsp herbes de Provence
- 1lemon, quartered
- 8 to 10cloves garlic, peeled
- 4 to 6medium-size shallots, peeled and halved
- ⅓cup of dry vermouth
- 4sprigs of thyme, for serving

PREPARATION

- Heat the oven to 400 degrees. Add salt and pepper to the chicken to season it. Shake the chicken pieces to reTransfer extra flour after lightly dredging them in a shallow flour pan.
- Add the floured chicken in a large roasPang pan and swirl in the oil. Herbes de Provence is used to season the chicken. Pour the vermouth into the pan after positioning the lemon, shallots, and garlic cloves around the chicken.
- After roasPang the pan in the oven for 25 to 30 minutes, bat it with the pan's juices. Bake the chicken for twenty to thirty minutes or Before the meat is cooked and the bird is exceptionally crisp.
- Garnish with the thyme and serve in the pan or a heated Bowl.

GRILLED SALMON WITH LEMON AND HERBS

Prep Time: 10mins | Cook Time: 20mins | Total Time: 30 Mins

INGREDIENTS

- 2 pounds salmon Chinook, Coho, and event Atlantic salmon all work well
- 1 tsp kosher salt
- ½ tsp ground black pepper
- 4 Tbsp (½ stick) unsalted butter, melted
- 2 garlic cloves, minced
- 1 large lemon, sliced thinly
- 1 Tbsp finely chopped fresh or dried dill

INSTRUCTION

- Adjust the grill's heat to medium. Sprinkle salt and pepper on the salmon's two sides.
- Arrange the salmon on a sizable sliver of metal foil suitable for encircling the fish.
- To prevent the subsequent ingredients from spilling out, raise the sides of the foil to form a barrier.
- Slowly cover the fish with melted butter.
- Evenly scatter chopped dill and minced garlic over the salmon.
- Lay slices of lemon on top of the fish.
- Gently fold the foil's corners and edges over the salmon. Just enough room should be left between the foil and the salmon's flesh so that it is wholly covered yet allows for some breathing room. Avoid packing it in too firmly. Additionally, leave a Pany gap at the top.
- Grill for fifteen to eighteen minutes over medium heat.

BAKED SEA BASS WITH VEGETABLES

Ready In: 50mins

INGREDIENTS

- 4filets sea bass (or a mild white flesh fish of your choice)
- 1onion, finely chopped
- 3garlic cloves, crushed and finely chopped
- 3medium tomatoes, finely chopped
- 2 -3medium potatoes, par boiled for 10 minutes
- 1/2lemon, juiced
- 1/4cup of water
- 4 tbsp. olive oil
- 1tsp red pepper flakes
- salt & fresh ground pepper
- 1/4cup of Italian parsley, coarsely chopped
- 4lemon wedges, to serve

DIRECTIONS

- Adjust oven temperature to 350F.
- After ten minutes of boiling, reTransfer the water and set aside to cool the potatoes. Cut potatoes in half and thinly slice once they are cool enough to handle.
- Warm up two tsp of olive oil as the potatoes boil in a large, sturdy skillet. Add the chopped onions and simmer, stirring, for 3 to 4 minutes or Before soft. Add the chopped garlic and tomatoes and simmer for three minutes on medium-low heat. The lemon juice and water should be added. For example, add freshly ground black pepper and salt seasoning. Simmer on low for an additional two minutes, then turn off the heat and let cool.
- After using the remaining two tbsp of olive oil to grease a baking sheet, add the fish fillets and potato slices to the Bowl and drizzle with olive oil. Add freshly ground black pepper and salt for seasoning.

- Arrange the fish fillets with the tomato and onion combination on top, and then arrange the potato slices on the side. Bake the baking Bowl in the oven for 20 to 25 minutes while covered with aluminum foil.
- After cooking, reTransfer the foil from the fish and top it with red pepper flakes and chopped parsley. Accompany the Bowl right away with lemon wedges on the side.

MEDITERRANEAN-STYLE COD FILLETS WITH OLIVES AND CAPERS

Prep Time: 10 minutes | Cook Time: 25 minutes | Total Time: 35 minutes

INGREDIENTS

- 4 frOuncesen cod fillets, thawed
- 3 tbsp evo oil
- a handful of roasted black olives
- a heaping tsp of capers
- 2 garlic cloves
- 8-10 cherry tomatoes, halved
- parsley, chopped
- a good pinch of salt
- a sprinkle of peperoncino (or pepper)

INSTRUCTIONS

- Before patPang dry with a paper towel, thaw your cod fillets.
- Give a baking Bowl a quick oiling. Line the oil with the fish fillets.
- Additional oil should be drizzled on top. Garlic cloves, capers, olives, halved cherry tomatoes, and salt and pepper (or peperoncino) can be used to season.
- Add some chopped parsley on top last.
- Fish thickness will determine how long to bake at 200°C/400°F, usually 20 to 25 minutes. Try basPang the fillets with their juices or add a splash of white wine and let it dissolve if it seems like they are becoming too dry.

PAN-SEARED TUNA STEAKS WITH "MELTED" LEMON-CAPER SAUCE

Prep Time: 10 Minutes | Cook Time: 18 Minutes| Total Time: 28 Minutes

INGREDIENTS

- 3 T. extra virgin olive oil, divided
- 4 6-Ounces. sushi-grade tuna steaks, approximately 3/4" thick
- Salt and black pepper, to taste

INSTRUCTIONS

- Warm up two tsp olive oil in a big skillet in a saucepan over medium-high heat. After adding the tuna steaks to the heated skillet, sauté them for about two minutes, or one minute on everyside for medium-rare.
- After flipping the tuna, taste and add salt and black pepper as needed. Depending on the desired doneness, cook for two to three minutes. When the tuna steaks are on a platter, season with black pepper and salt, if preferred. Stay warm.
- Pour the leftover olive oil and the chopped shallots into the skillet. Add the shallots and sauté, stirring periodically, Before soft and beginning to turn golden brown, about 3 minutes.
- Add lemon juice, white wine, chicken stock, and lemon slices to the skillet. Using a spatula, scrape off any brown bits to deglaze it; start at the bottom of the pan. Cook Before the liquid is reduced by half, stirring constantly.
- Turn down to medium and stir in capers. Cook for a Another minute or Before well cooked, stirring to mix.
- Place the tuna steaks onto separate serving Bowles, garnish with a slice of "melted" lemon and a dollop of the lemon-caper sauce, and serve immediately with your preferred sides. Have fun!

MEDITERRANEAN FISH SOUP WITH SAFFRON AND GARLIC TOAST

Prep Time: 10 minutes | Cook Time: 30 minutes | Total Time: 40 minutes

INGREDIENTS

For the soup:

- 1 medium onion
- 5 garlic cloves
- 2 tbsp extra virgin olive oil
- a good pinch of hot pepper flakes
- 1 cup of white wine
- A good pinch of saffron
- 1½ cup of canned crushed tomatoes
- 1 quart fish stock
- 1 15- ounce cans of white beans
- 1½ pound meaty fish fillets
- Parsley for garnish.
- For the garlic toasts:
- 1 baguette
- Extra virgin olive oil
- 1 garlic clove

INSTRUCTIONS

- Over medium heat, heat a soup pot or Dutch oven. Dice the onion, reTransfer the skin, and cut four garlic cloves while it's heaPang up; save the other clove whole for later.
- Add the hot pepper flakes, olive oil, onions, and garlic to the pot, and a pinch of salt and black pepper once heated.
- Cook the onions Before they are soft but not brown, stirring occasionally.
- After adding the wine, carefully scrape any bits off the pan's bottom using a wooden spoon. The saffron should be added to the bubbling wine and gently stirred to allow the saffron to dissolve into the wine. Add a little salt and pepper

along with the tomatoes and fish stock. Once the soup reaches a boiling point, Simmer it for 10 minutes with a lid on low heat.

- Prepare the additional ingredients while the soup cooks. Rinse and drain the beans, then cut the fish into large slices. Cut a few beautiful, angled slices of bread, peel the last garlic clove, and prepare a small basin with a brush and olive oil.

- Add the beans and fish to the saucepan, and simmer for 4–5 minutes, based on the fish's thickness, or Before the fish is finished. As you serve it, it will keep cooking.

- As the fish cooks, toast the bread pieces Before crisp by brushing them with olive oil, cut a clove of garlic in half, then gently massage the garlic over the bread.

- Spoon soup into bowls. Serve the garlic toast beside the garnish of parsley.

GRILLED SARDINES WITH GARLIC OLIVE OIL AND LEMON

Prep Time: 20 Minutes | Cooking Time: 20 Minutes

INGREDIENTS

- 4 Butterflied Sardines
- 4 Garlic cloves crushed
- Extra Virgin olive oil
- ½ tbsp Lemon zest
- 2 tbsp Lemon juice
- Small handful coriander
- ½ tsp Sweet smoked paprika
- Sea salt
- Freshly ground black pepper
- 3 Tomatoes sliced
- 1 Shallot chopped fine
- 1 lemon halved (optional)
- Small handful fresh parsley chopped

INSTRUCTIONS

- Turn on your oven's grill.
- Crushed garlic, lemon zest, lemon juice, coriander, paprika, salt, and pepper should all be mixd to make a paste with around 100ml of olive oil.
- Sardines should be placed skin-side up on an oven tray and slathered with paste.
- Fish should be baked for 5 to 8 minutes or Before crispy skins are cooked. Then, reTransfer and set aside.
- If using a grill, coat the cut side of the lemon halves with olive oil before placing them under the heat source Before they are browned. As an alternative, cook on a BBQ or grill pan Before blackened.
- Arrange the tomato slices on a Bowl or serving board.
- Sprinkle the finely chopped parsley and shallots on top, then pour EVOO and a squeeze of lemon over everything.
- Top the sliced tomatoes with the sardines and their spicy juices.
- If desired, garnish with charred lemon halves.
- Serve hot with a large green salad and toasted bread.

BAKED TROUT WITH LEMON AND DILL

Prep Time: 10 mins | Cook Time:25 mins | Total Time: 35 mins

INGREDIENTS

- 2 (½-pound) trout, entrails reTransferd and the trout cleaned well under fresh, cold water
- ½ tbsp olive oil
- ½ tsp salt
- ½ tsp freshly ground black pepper
- ½ tsp dried dill (dill weed)
- ¼ tsp onion powder
- 4 to 6 sprigs fresh dill
- 2 lemons, one thinly sliced with seeds reTransferd and the other cut into wedges to serve with the baked fish

INSTRUCTIONS

- Set the oven's temperature to 400 degrees. Place parchment paper into a sheet pan and set it aside.
- Get the trout ready: After removing the trout's entrails and cleaning it, pat it dry using paper towels to eliminate any remaining dampness.
- **Note:** The goal is to open the fish's body cavity so that you can fill and season it. Cut it in half lengthwise, leaving the two sides intact.
- **Note:** You are free to reTransfer the trout heads if you choose. ReTransfer the gills before using if the head is left on.
- Toss the trout in season: Add a little layer of olive oil on the exterior of every trout. Use onion powder, dried dill, black pepper, and salt to season the inside of everytrout. Place dill sprigs into the cavity and cover the dill with lemon slices (save 2 to 4 for the top of the trout). After stuffing, place one or two lemon slices on top of everytrout.
- **Note:** Go ahead and eat the fish skin if you'd like! I don't. Just before you place the lemon slices on top, season with salt & pepper outside.

- Cooking the trout involves baking it for 22 to 25 minutes, or Before it is cooked through, the meat is opaque, and it flakes readily when a fork is inserted into the thickest portion of the fish and pulled back.
- **Note:** Depending on the size of your trout, the cooking time may change.
- Squeeze lemon wedges over the fish before serving it. It should be simple to separate the flesh from the skin. ReTransfer the bones and consume the meat surrounding them. Have fun!

GRILLED SWORDFISH TOASTS WITH LEMON-OLIVE TAPENADE

Total Time: 30 Mins

INGREDIENTS

- 4 swordfish steaks (about 6 Ounces. each), dark portions reTransferd
- 6 tbsp olive oil, divided
- Salt and pepper to taste
- 4 slices rustic white bread cut from a loaf
- 1/4 cup of pitted Castelvetrano or other mild green olives
- 2 to 3 tbsp. harissa* (North African chile-and-spice paste)
- 2 tbsp chopped preserved lemon
- 1 large garlic clove
- 2 cup ofs of kale leaves, shredded

HOW TO MAKE IT

- Grill on medium-high heat (500°). Swordfish steaks should be seasoned with salt and pepper and brushed with one tbsp of oil—Grill for 3 to 4 minutes on everyside or Before cooked through, flipping once. While waiPang, lightly toast the bread on the grill for one to two minutes on everyside, brushing it with one tbsp of oil. Place the bread and fish on a platter.
- **Prepare the tapenade:** Blend the olives, harissa, garlic, preserved lemon, and the remaining 1/4 cup of oil in a blender for approximately 15 seconds or Before almost smooth. After spreading roughly one tbsp of tapenade on

everyslice of bread, add swordfish and kale on top. You can find Containers or bowles of harissa in well-stocked supermarket stores.

RED SNAPPER WITH CITRUS AND FENNEL SALAD

Total Time: 40 mins | Yield: 4

INGREDIENTS

- 4 small raBowles, thinly sliced
- 1/2 small fennel bulb—halved, cored and shaved paper-thin
- 1/2 small red or yellow bell pepper, finely diced
- 1 jalapeño, seeded and thinly sliced
- 1/4 cup of coarsely chopped cilantro
- 1 tbsp snipped chives
- 1 tbsp finely shredded mint leaves
- 1 grapefruit
- 1 navel orange
- 2 tbsp extra-virgin olive oil, + more for brushing
- 1 tbsp fresh lemon juice
- Salt and freshly ground pepper
- Four 6-ounce skinless red snapper fillets

DIRECTIONS

- Set the broiler to high. Mix the raBowles, fennel, bell pepper, jalapeño, cilantro, chives, and mint in a big basin. Peel the orange and grapefruit with a sharp knife, eliminaPang all the bitter white pith. Cut through the membranes while working over the bowl to release the portions. Over the bowl, squeeze the membranes. Toss in the two tbsp of olive oil; add the salt, squeeze in the lemon juice, and pepper to taste.
- Place the fish on a baking sheet that has been well-oiled and generously brushed with olive oil. Season with salt and pepper. Just Before completely white, broil 6 inches from the heat for 4 minutes, only on one side. Transfer the fish to plates using a spatula. Place the salad on top and serve.

TUNA STEAK WITH CAPONATA

Total Time: 45 mins

INGREDIENTS

For 4 People

- 1 lb tuna
- 3 ½ Ounces onion
- 3 ½ Ounces eggplant
- 3 ½ Ounces zucchini
- 3 ½ Ounces red pepper
- 1 Ounces raisins
- 1 Ounces pine nuts
- 1 Ounces pistachios
- 1 tbsp white balsamic vinegar
- 1 Ounces sugar
- 1 clove of garlic
- 1 pinch salt
- black pepper to taste
- extra virgin olive oil to taste

PREPARATION

- Traditionally, eggplants are deep-fried with caponata to enhance their flavor.
- Only at the very end are cubes of deep-fried eggplant added to the other components.
- A Pany bit of extra virgin olive oil should be added to a frying pan, and begin to sauté the red onion, red pepper, and zucchini in order of preference.
- The deep-fried eggplant, capers, sultanas, pine nuts, sugar, white vinegar, and pistachios can all be added after three or four minutes.
- When the caponata is done, set it aside warmly before proceeding with the tuna steak.
- For the tuna steak to be seared appropriately, it must be at least one inch thick.
- Add salt and pepper to the meat before cooking it.

- Place extra virgin olive oil from Italy in a frying pan, add some crushed garlic (which you will reTransfer later), and sear the tuna steak for about a minute on everyside.
- The tuna steak can be served whole or sliced after it has been seared.
- As a last step in preparation and serving advice, place the sliced seared tuna steak on one side of the Bowl and serve the caponata on the other using a Pan stamp.

FISH TAGINE WITH TOMATOES, OLIVES AND PRESERVED LEMON

Cooking Time: 1 hour 10 minutes

INGREDIENTS

FOR THE CHARMOULA:

- 2 tsp cumin seeds
- 3 cloves garlic
- 1 tsp coarse salt
- 1 tbsp sweet paprika
- 1 ½ tsp crushed hot red pepper
- 2 tbsp coarsely chopped fresh flat-leaf parsley
- 2 tbsp chopped fresh cilantro
- 4 wedges preserved lemons, rinsed, pulp and peel separated
- 3 tbsp fruity extra-virgin olive oil
- FOR THE FISH TAGINE:
- 1 pound monkfish fillet or thick slabs of halPoundsut
- 1 large carrot, very thinly sliced in a diagonal
- 2 rPoundss celery, peeled and very thinly sliced
- 1 pound red ripe tomatoes, peeled and thinly sliced
- 1 small green bell pepper, sliced into very thin rounds
- 2 dOuncesen Moroccan red or picholine olives, rinsed and pitted
- 2 dried bay leaves, preferably Turkish

- Sprigs fresh cilantro, for garnish

INSTRUCTIONS

Heat a small skillet over medium heat to make the chermoula. Once the cumin seeds are aromatic and toasted, add them and ground them into a fine powder. Add the cumin to a mortar or blender Container with olive oil, garlic, paprika, parsley, cilantro, and preserved lemon pulp. Puree with a pestle and mortar or mix to produce a chermoula.

Marinate the fish:

- After rinsing, pat the fish dry.
- ReTransfer the gray membrane from the monkfish and cut it into four equal pieces.
- Add half of the chermoula to the fish and let it stand at room temperature for an hour or in the refrigerator for up to 24 hours.
- To the remaining Charmoula, add 1/2 cup of water, cover, and refrigerate.

Turn the oven on to 300°F. Line a tagine with two tbsp of the reserved chermoula and top with carrots and celery. Add half the bell peppers and tomatoes; sprinkle some Charmoula over the fish. Top with remaining chermoula and add remaining tomatoes and bell peppers. Chop the preserved lemon peel and scatter the olives and bay leaves on the fish.

Bake the fish tagine: Bake the tagine for an hour, covered with aluminum foil lined with parchment paper.

Reduce the sauce by removing the tagine from the oven and adding the liquid to a small, non-reactive pot. Re-pour over fish after bringing to a boil over medium-high heat and reducing to 1/2 cup of thickened liquid.

End bake:

- Raise the oven's setPang to 425°F.
- Brush the fish with the liquids from the pan and bake it uncovered in the upper third of the oven for about ten minutes or Before a crust forms over the veggies.
- Transfer the tagine on a hardwood surface or place it on a folded kitchen towel to stop it from Cup ofang.
- Garnish with sprigs of cilantro and serve hot or warm.

SHRIMP SAGANAKI (GREEK SHRIMP WITH TOMATOES & FETA)

Prep Time: 10 Minutes | Cook Time: 40 Minutes | Total Time: 50 Minutes

INGREDIENTS

- ¼ cup of extra-virgin olive oil
- ¾ cup of finely chopped shallots, from about 3 shallots
- 4 garlic cloves, roughly chopped
- 1 (28-Ounces) can diced tomatoes
- 1½ tsp salt
- ¼ tsp pepper
- 1 tsp ground cumin
- ½ tsp crushed red pepper flakes (use less if you are heat-sensitive)
- 1 tbsp honey
- 1½ pounds extra large shrimp (26/30), peeled and deveined, thawed if frOuncesen
- 6 ounces feta cheese
- ¾ tsp dried oregano
- 2 tbsp roughly chopped fresh mint

INSTRUCTIONS

- Set one oven rack in the center and another approximately 5 inches beneath the broiler after preheaPang the oven to 400°F.
- In a big pot, heat the olive oil over medium-low heat ovenproof skillet (see note). Stirring occasionally, add the shallots and garlic, and simmer for 5 to 7 minutes or Before softened. Avoid browning.
- Add the red pepper flakes, honey, cumin, salt, pepper, and tomatoes with their juices. Once it reaches a boiling point, lower the heat to medium-low and simmer for 15 to 20 minutes without a lid, stirring Before the sauce thickens.
- Turn off the heat and spread an even layer of shrimp over the tomato sauce. After crumbling the feta over the shrimp, scatter the oregano on top. Shrimp should be baked for 12 to 15 minutes, depending on their size, or Before they

are pink and cooked through. Activate the broiler. Spoon the pan onto the higher oven rack with care, using an oven mitt, and broil for 1 to 2 minutes or Before the feta starts to become golden brown. Using an oven mitt, reTransfer the pan; quickly cover the pan's handle with a Bowltowel or the mitt because it's easy to forget that it's pretty hot. After giving the shrimp five minutes to rest, garnish with mint and serve.

- Note: You can Transfer the tomato sauce to a 9-by-13-inch or similar broiler-safe baking Bowl and conPanue if you don't have an ovenproof skillet.

GRILLED ANCHOVIES WITH FRESH SUMMER DRESSING

Prep Time: 15 Minutes | Cook Time:5 Minutes

INGREDIENTS

- 500 grams fresh anchovies, cleaned and cut in half
- 1 piece large tomato
- 1 piece garlic clove
- 1 tbsp chopped fresh parsley
- 1/2 tsp fresh thyme
- 1/4 cup of lime juice
- 2 tbsp lemon juice
- 2 tbsp olive oil
- 1/2 tsp sea salt
- 1/4 tsp black pepper

DIRECTIONS

- 1/4 tsp of olive oil should be heated in a big skillet or grill pan.
- Lay the anchovies flat in the skillet, skin side up, while working in batches. After cooking for a minute on everyside, place on a Bowl.
- New summer attire: Tomatoes should be cut into small cubes and Add in a bowl.
- Grate or chop the garlic finely, then add it to the bowl with the tomato.

- Add the olive oil, salt, pepper, lemon and lime juice, parsley, and thyme. Blend thoroughly.
- Serve it with lime slices on top of the grilled anchovies. Have fun!

LEMON HERB GRILLED CHICKEN

Prep Time: 1hr | Cook Time:15mins | Total Time: 1hr 15mins

INGREDIENTS

- 2 lbs chicken breasts, trimmed
- LEMON HERB MARINADE
- 1/4 cup of olive oil, extra virgin
- 1/4 cup of lemon juice
- 1 tbsp dried basil
- 1 tbsp dried parsley
- 1 tsp salt
- 1/2 tsp black pepper
- 1/2 tsp garlic powder
- 1/2 tsp onion powder
- 1/4 tsp crushed red pepper flakes

INSTRUCTIONS

- Add the ingredients for the lemon herb marinade in a gallon-sized Ziploc bag along with your chicken breasts. Seal the bag after squeezing out any leftover air. Give the chicken a minimum of one hour and twelve hours to marinate.
- Depending on your taste, you can either grill or sauté your chicken. Below are the instructions for both.
- GRILLING
- Take everychicken breast from the bag and set everyover medium heat on a heated grill. Grill Before done, 5 to 7 minutes on everyside. (Juices ought to flow freely.)
- ABOVE THE STOVE
- Warm up two tsp of olive oil or frying fat in a pan. Oil is heated to a medium-high temperature. (When the chicken sizzles as you Add it in the pan, you know

it's ready.) Place a single layer of chicken breasts in the skillet. Simmer for around five minutes. Turn over your chicken. Simmer for five more minutes. When the chicken is done, its fluids should run clear and firm to the touch.

MEDITERRANEAN BEEF STEW AND GREEN OLIVES

Prep time:20minutes | Cook time:1hour | Total time:1hour 20minutes

INGREDIENTS

- 1 pound Beef cheek meat, sliced (or shoulder roast)
- 6-8 ounces green olives
- 30 ounces tomato sauce
- 4 ounces tomato paste
- 4 cloves garlic (sliced or minced)
- 1 large onion, sliced (white, yellow or red)
- 2 bay leaves
- ½ tsp thyme (dried or chopped)
- ½ tsp oregano (dried or chopped)
- ¼ tsp rosemary (dried or chopped)
- ½ tsp salt
- ¼ tsp black pepper, ground
- 2-3 dried guajillo peppers (whole)
- ¼ cup of olive oil

INSTRUCTIONS

- Transfer the olive oil into a big pot and set it over medium heat.
- Add the beef, garlic, guajillo peppers, olives, and chopped onions. Fry, stirring, Before onions become soft.
- Stir in tomato paste and tomato sauce Before well mixd. After adding all of the spices, cover. Simmer for 60 minutes at low to medium heat, stirring occasionally.
- Serve hot over pasta or rice or as a stew.

FENNEL-GARLIC PORK ROAST

Active Time:45 mins | Total Time:4 hrs

INGREDIENTS

- Brine
- 1/4 cup of honey
- 2 tbsp black peppercorns
- 18 fresh bay leaves (1/3 ounce)
- 10 thyme sprigs
- 10 flat-leaf parsley sprigs
- 2 heads of garlic, halved horizontally
- 1 cup of kosher salt
- 3 quarts cold water
- One 4-pound boneless pork loin, tied
- Rub
- 2 tbsp fennel seeds, coarsely chopped
- 1 tsp crushed red pepper
- 6 garlic cloves, thinly sliced
- 1 tsp finely grated lemon zest
- Pinch of salt
- 1/4 cup of extra-virgin olive oil
- 2 tbsp canola oil

DIRECTIONS

- Prepare the brine.
- Add the honey, peppercorns, bay leaves, thyme, parsley, garlic, and salt in a medium saucepan with one quart of water. Increase heat to a boil and whisk to dissolve the salt. Transfer the brine to a big bowl and let it cool. After adding the pork and the remaining 2 quarts of cold water, cover and chill for 12 to 18 hours. After draining, pat dry and reTransfer any seasonings.
- Create the Rub

- Process or pound the fennel seeds and red pepper; mix the garlic, lemon zest, and salt using a small food processor or mortar. Add the olive oil and stir. After Adding half of the spice paste on the lean side of the pork, leave it for two hours at room temperature.
- Adjust an oven rack to a sizeable rimmed bake sheet and set the oven temperature to 350°. Heat the canola oil on a giant grill Before it shimmers. Add the pork and fat side down and cook for about five minutes over moderately high heat or Before browned. Place the pork on the rack, skin side up, and generously coat with the leftover garlic paste. Roast the pork for approximately one hour or Before the thickest section registers 140° to 145° on an instant-read thermometer Add into it. Before slicing, let it rest for twenty minutes.

SOUTZOUKAKIA: GREEK BAKED MEATBALLS IN TOMATO SAUCE

Prep: 20 Mins | cook: 1Hr 40Mins

INGREDIENTS

For Meatballs

- 2 slices whole wheat bread, toast-size, toasted to a medium-brown (or use gluten free bread if you need)
- ⅓ cup of whole milk
- 1.5 pounds lean ground beef
- 1 small yellow onion, chopped
- 3 garlic cloves, minced
- 2 medium eggs
- 1 tsp ground cumin
- ½ tsp ground cinnamon
- ½ tsp dried oregano
- ½ cup of chopped fresh parsley
- Kosher salt and black pepper
- Extra virgin olive oil, to grease the baking Bowl

- For Red Sauce
- 2 tbsp Extra virgin olive oil
- 1 medium yellow onion, finely chopped
- 2 garlic cloves, minced
- ½ cup of dry red wine
- 30 ounces canned tomato sauce, that's 2 15-ounce cans of sauce
- 1 bay leaf
- ¾ tsp ground cumin
- ½ tsp cinnamon
- ½ tsp sugar
- Kosher salt and black pepper

INSTRUCTIONS

- Toasted bread should be placed in a small basin and soaked with milk (or water). Squeeze out the liquid once the bread is soft and adequately soaked, and discard any leftover milk.
- The bread should be Transferd to a sizable mixing bowl. Stir in the other meatball ingredients and the ground beef. Mix thoroughly Before thoroughly mixed. For the time being, cover and refrigerate the beef mixture.
- Turn the oven on to 400°F.
- Make the sauce while the oven heats. Two tbsp of extra virgin olive oil should be heated over medium heat in a saucepan or big skillet Before shimmering but not smoking. Add the onions and simmer for about three minutes. Cook the garlic for a Another minute while stirring frequently. After adding the red wine and letPang it reduce by roughly ½, add the tomato sauce, bay leaf, and the additional ingredients for the sauce. Heat till boiling, then reduce the temperature to simmer for fifteen minutes.
- Add a modest quantity of extra virgin olive oil to the top of a big baking Bowl.
- ReTransfer the beef mixture from the refrigerator. Using damp hands, take approximately ½ tbsp of the meat mixture and shape it into big, long meatballs that resemble footballs. There should be about 15 to 16 meatballs in total. Place the meatballs in the baking Bowl lined with parchment paper, then cover with the sauce (making sure the sauce has been strained of the bay leaf).
- After preheaPang your oven, place the baking Bowl on the middle shelf. Bake the meatballs for 40 to 45 minutes, or Before they are well cooked (check

halfway through to ensure the sauce is not drying up, and add a small amount of water to the bottom of the baking Bowl if necessary).

- Take out of the oven and pour some more EVOO on top. Serve with orzo or rice and garnish with parsley.

STUFFED PEPPERS WITH GROUND BEEF AND RICE

Prep:25 Mins | Cook: 85 Mins | Total:110 Mins

INGREDIENTS

- 6 green bell peppers (or choose a combination of colors)
- 1 tbsp extra-virgin olive oil
- 1 tbsp unsalted butter
- 1/2 cup of chopped onion
- 1/2 cup of chopped celery
- 1 (14.5-ounce) can diced tomatoes
- 1 (8-ounce) can tomato sauce
- 1 clove garlic, crushed and minced
- 1 tsp dried oregano
- 1/2 tsp dried basil
- 2 tsp kosher salt, divided
- 1/2 tsp ground black pepper, divided
- 1 large egg, lightly beaten
- 1 1/2 tsp Worcestershire sauce
- 1 1/2 pounds lean ground beef (90/10)
- 1 1/2 cup ofs of cooked long-grain rice
- Shredded mild cheddar cheese (about 1/2 to 3/4 cup of), optional

STEPS TO MAKE IT

- Collect the necessary components.
- ReTransfer the top part of the bell peppers and wash them with cold water; discard the seeds and the bitter white rPoundss. Separate the edPoundsle

portion of the tops and place it aside. Transfer the peppers to a spacious pot and submerge them in water seasoned with salt.

- Add heat Before the liquid reaches the state of boiling. Turn down the heat, place a lid on the pot, and let it cook gently for 5 minutes. ReTransfer the liquid and Add it in a separate container.

- They were warming up butter and olive oil in a spacious skillet on medium heat Before the oil was heated and the butter became frothy. Cook the diced bell pepper (from the tops), diced onion, and chopped celery in a hot pan for approximately 5 minutes or Before the vegetables are soft.

- Incorporate the canned diced tomatoes (without draining), tomato sauce, crushed garlic, oregano, basil, one tsp of salt, and 1/4 tsp of pepper. Add heat to the mixture Before it reaches a mild boiling state and conPanue cooking for approximately 10 minutes.

- In a large mixing bowl, incorporate the egg with the remaining one-quarter tsp of pepper and salt—Worcestershire sauce. Stir gently to mix; mix ground meat; mix cooked rice with 1 cup of of tomato sauce. Thoroughly mix the ingredients.

- Heat the oven to 350 degrees Fahrenheit.

- Stuff the combination of ground beef into the peppers. Loosely Add them in a baking tray measuring 13 x 9 x 2 inches. Drizzle the remaining tomato mixture onto the filled peppers.

- Cook the peppers in the oven for approximately 45 minutes or Before the meat filling is thoroughly cooked.

Prep Time:10 Minutes | Cook Time:35 Minutes | Total Time:45 Minutes

INGREDIENTS

- 1 large head cauliflower, cut into florets (about 4-5 cup ofs of cauliflower florets)
- 3 tbsp olive oil, divided
- Freshly ground salt and pepper
- 1 head garlic
- 1 medium yellow onion, diced
- 4 cup ofs of vegetable broth (or sub chicken broth if not vegetarian)*
- ½ tsp salt, + more to taste
- Freshly ground black pepper
- 1 heaping cup of shredded sharp cheddar cheese
- To garnish:
- Sliced green onion & extra cheddar on top
- Croutons or toasted sourdough bread/bread of choice for dipping/serving

INSTRUCTIONS

- Set the oven temperature to 400°F before baking. Ensure that parchment paper is used to line a baking sheet.
- Prepare the vegetables: When the cauliflower florets are added to the skillet, stir them together after lPoundserally seasoning with salt and pepper and drizzling with one or two tbsp of olive oil. Regarding the garlic, reTransfer the outer papery layers from the entire head and dispose of them. Everyclove should retain its skin intact. Cut a quarter of an inch off the top of everygarlic clove with a sharp knife to reveal the individual cloves. Garlic should be placed in a medium-sized piece of foil, covered loosely with the foil, and placed on the pan with the cauliflower after drizzling with olive oil. Garlic and cauliflower should be roasted for 30 to 35 minutes, turning the cauliflower halfway through or Before the cauliflower is nicely caramelized and brown.

- Cook the onion: Add one tbsp of olive oil in a pot and set it over medium heat while the cauliflower cooks. The diced onion should be added to hot oil and sautéed for 5 to 8 minutes or Before transparent.
- Place the onion, roasted cauliflower, garlic, broth, salt, and pepper in a large blender to mix the soup. After blending for one minute or Before smooth, return to the pot and set over medium heat. For the garlic, squeeze the roasted garlic from its skin after letPang it cool enough to touch.
- To sum it up: After bringing the soup to a gentle simmer, mix in the cheddar cheese; after ten to fifteen minutes of simmering, taste and adjust the seasonings. Add some more shredded sharp cheddar cheese and green onions as garnish. Serve with your favorite bread or with crusty toasted sourdough.

LENTIL SOUP WITH LEMON AND TURMERIC

Prep Time: 10mins | Cook Time: 50mins | Total: 1hr

INGRIDIENTS

- 2 tbsp olive oil
- 2 cup ofs of finely chopped onion (1 medium onion)
- 1 1/2 cup ofs of chopped carrot (2 large carrots)
- 2 tsp minced garlic (3 cloves)
- 1 tsp ground cumin
- 1/2 tsp ground coriander
- 1/2 tsp fresh ground black pepper
- 1/2 tsp ground turmeric
- 2 cup ofs of (12 ounces) lentils, picked and rinsed
- 8 cup ofs of chicken or vegetable brot
- 2 heaping cup ofs of shredded kale or spinach
- 1 to 2 lemons
- 1/4 cup of chopped fresh herbs like parsley or dill, optional
- Fine sea salt, to taste

DIRECTIONS

- 1Heat the oil in a big saucepan over medium heat, such as a Dutch oven. When the onions, carrot, and 1/4 tsp of salt are added, simmer them for 5 to 7 minutes, stirring now and again, Before they are softened and beginning to smell pleasant. Add the turmeric, black pepper, cumin, coriander, and garlic; heat for 30 seconds.
- 2Incorporate the lentils and stock. Just bring it to a boil after turning the heat up to high. After tasPang the soup, we add salt to taste (we usually add 1/2 to 1 tsp, depending on how seasoned the broth is). After lowering the heat to a simmer, cook the lentils for 35 to 40 minutes with a partially covered Bowl Before they are cooked.
- 3Take off the lid, add the spinach or kale, and simmer for five minutes. After turning off the heat, whisk in the fresh herbs and the juice from half a lemon. To taste, increase the salt or lemon juice in the soup and adjust the seasoning. (I enjoy lemon quite a bit.)
- 4Serve or, if you'd instead, puree the soup with an immersion blender to the appropriate smoothness. Alternatively, puree some or all of the soup in a stand blender. Serve with a few lemon slices for extra lemon flavor.

ITALIAN ORZO SPINACH SOUP

Prep Time: 5 Minutes | Cook Time: 25 Minutes | Total Time: 30 Minutes

INGREDIENTS

- 1 tbsp olive oil
- 1 small white onion, peeled and diced
- 1 cup of diced carrots
- 1 cup of diced celery
- 6 cloves garlic, pressed or minced
- 1/2 tsp crushed red pepper flakes
- 6 to 8 cup ofs of chicken or vegetable stock
- 1 (14-ounce) can fire-roasted diced tomatoes
- 1 1/2 tbsp Italian seasoning
- 1 cup of (about 8 ounces) uncooked orzo pasta

- 2 large handfuls fresh baby spinach or kale
- fine sea salt and freshly-cracked black pepper
- optional toppings: freshly-grated Parmesan cheese and/or chopped fresh basil

INSTRUCTIONS

- Saute the vegetables. The oil should be warmed in a medium-high heat big saucepan stock pot. Stirring periodically, sauté the onion, carrots, and celery for 5-7 minutes Before they become soft. Simmer the garlic for two minutes, stirring often, while adding the crushed red pepper flakes.
- Melt slowly. Stir to mix the stock, diced tomatoes, and Italian seasoning. Reduce heat to medium-low to keep the broth simmering after cooking Before it reaches a simmer.
- Sauté the orzo. Once mixed, stir in the orzo. The orzo should be barely dente, so cover the pot and boil the soup for a little longer, stirring now and then so as not to allow the orzo to adhere to the bottom. (Aim to cook the orzo sparingly!
- Mix in the spinach and season. Pour the soup with the spinach and stir. Use salt and black pepper to taste and adjust the seasoning.
- Add to use. Add your preferred toppings on top and serve right away to savor!

CLASSIC MINESTRONE SOUP

Prep Time: 20 minutes | Cook Time: 45 minutes | Total Time: 1 hour 5 minutes

INGREDIENTS

- 4 tbsp extra-virgin olive oil, divided
- 1 medium yellow onion, chopped
- 2 medium carrots, peeled and chopped
- 2 medium rPoundss celery, chopped
- ¼ cup of tomato paste
- 2 cup ofs of chopped seasonal vegetables (potatoes, yellow squash, zucchini, butternut squash, green beans or peas all work)
- 4 cloves garlic, pressed or minced
- ½ tsp dried oregano

- ½ tsp dried thyme
- 1 large can (28 ounces) diced tomatoes, with their liquid (or 2 small 15-ounce cans)
- 4 cup ofs of (32 ounces) vegetable broth
- 2 cup ofs of water
- 1 tsp fine sea salt
- 2 bay leaves
- Pinch of red pepper flakes
- Freshly ground black pepper
- 1 cup of whole grain orecchiette, elbow or small shell pasta
- 1 can (15 ounces) Great Northern beans or cannellini beans, rinsed and drained, or 1 ½ cup ofs of cooked beans
- 2 cup ofs of baby spinach, chopped kale or chopped collard greens
- 2 tsp lemon juice
- Freshly grated Parmesan cheese, for garnishing (optional)

INSTRUCTIONS

- Warm three tbsp of olive oil using a medium-sized stockpot or Dutch oven. Add chopped tomato paste, celery, carrot, onion, and a dash of salt once the oil shatters. Simmer the vegetables for 7 to 10 minutes, stirring frequently, or Before they are soft and the onions become transparent.
- Garlic, oregano, thyme, and seasonal veggies should be added. Cook, stirring conPanually, for approximately two minutes or Before aromatiCup of
- Add the chopped tomatoes with their juices, water, and broth—season with the salt, red pepper flakes, and bay leaves. Give everything a good pinch of freshly ground black pepper.
- After bringing the mixture to a boil and increasing the heat to medium-high, partially cover the pot with the lid, leaving approximately a 1-inch space open to allow steam to escape to maintain a gentle simmer; adjust the heat as needed.
- After 15 minutes of cooking, take off the top and add the pasta, beans, and greens. After the pasta is cooked al dente and the greens are soft, simmer the mixture, uncovered, for an additional 20 minutes.
- After turning off the heat, reTransfer the bay leaves from the saucepan. Incorporate the lemon juice and the leftover tbsp of olive oil. Once the flavors

are genuinely pronounced, taste and add extra salt (I usually add approximately ¼ tsp more) and pepper. If desired, top soup Bowles with grated Parmesan cheese.

LEMON CHICKEN ORZO SOUP

Prep: 10 mins | Cook: 40 mins | Total: 50 mins | Servings: 6

INGREDIENTS

- 2 sticks celery chopped finely
- 2 medium carrots peeled & chopped finely
- 1/2 medium onion chopped
- 1 tbsp butter
- 1 tbsp olive oil
- 3 cloves garlic minced
- 2 tbsp flour
- 6 cup ofs of chicken broth
- 1/4 tsp Italian seasoning
- 1.5 pounds uncooked chicken breasts
- 1 cup of uncooked orzo
- 1 tbsp lemon juice or to taste
- 1 tbsp chopped fresh parsley or to taste
- Salt & pepper to taste

INSTRUCTIONS

- In a large soup pot, sauté the onions, carrots, and celery for five to seven minutes over medium-high heat with butter and oil.
- Cook for a minute more after adding the flour or stirring in the garlic and cooking for approximately 30 seconds.
- Once the flour has dissolved, pour in the chicken stock and stir. Next, add the chicken and Italian spice. Heat the soup Before it boils.

- Lower the heat and simmer it for fifteen minutes after covering the soup with the lid slightly aContainer.
- After adding the orzo, simmer for ten minutes or Before thoroughly cooked. It sticks to the bottom of the pot, so I keep the lid off and stir it rather frequently.
- ReTransfer and chop the chicken from the pot, then return it to the pot. Add the parsley and lemon juice (you might want to add more than I recommend because I wouldn't say I liked the soup to be very lemony for some people). When making the soup, add salt and pepper to taste. Assist right away.

MEDITERRANEAN FISH SOUP WITH SAFFRON AND GARLIC TOAST

Prep Time: 10 minutes | Cook Time: 30 minutes | Total Time: 40 minutes

INGREDIENTS

For the soup:

- 1 medium onion
- 5 garlic cloves
- 2 tbsp extra virgin olive oil
- a good pinch of hot pepper flakes
- 1 cup of white wine
- A good pinch of saffron
- 1½ cup of canned crushed tomatoes
- 1 quart fish stock
- 1 15- ounce cans of white beans
- 1½ pound meaty fish fillets
- Parsley for garnish.
- For the garlic toasts:
- 1 baguette
- Extra virgin olive oil
- 1 garlic clove

INSTRUCTIONS

- Set a Dutch oven or soup pot on medium heat. Chop the onion and four garlic cloves (keeping the other clove whole for later) while the pan is heaPang up.
- Add the garlic, onions, and hot pepper flakes to the heated pot, along with a pinch of salt and black pepper.
- Simmer the onions for a few minutes, stirring now and then, Before they are soft but not brown.
- Using a wooden spoon, incorporate the wine and stir to carefully scrape up any bits from the bottom of the pan. Add the saffron to the simmering wine and swirl slowly to allow the saffron to dissolve into the wine. Along with some salt and pepper, add the tomatoes and the fish stock. After bringing the soup, please boil it to a low simmer for 10 minutes while covered.
- Prepare the other ingredients while the soup is cooking. After slicing the fish into bite-sized pieces, drain and rinse the beans. Trim the remaining garlic clove, cut some beautiful baguette slices at an angle, and prepare olive oil in a little Bowl with a brush.
- When the fish is slightly underdone, add the beans to the saucepan and cook for 4–5 minutes, depending on the thickness of the fish. As you serve it, the cooking process will conPanue.
- Toast the bread pieces to crisp while the fish is cooking, brushing them with olive oil. Halve the garlic clove and Add the clove to the bread.
- Spoon soup into individual Bowles. Serve with the garlic toast and sprinkle the parsley on top.
- Such as lobster tail, cannellini, or great northern, including cod, salmon, halPoundsut, and any shellfish.

CRETAN BEAN SOUP (FASOLADA.)

Prep Time:10 Min | Cook Time:2 H 50 Min

INGREDIENTS

- 227 gr ½ lbs dried navy beans, picked over and rinsed
- 1 cup of extra virgin Greek olive oil
- 1 ½ cup ofs of red onion finely chopped
- 1 cup of finely chopped celery with leaves or ¾ cup of chopped wild celery sometimes called Chinese celery with leaves
- 1 large carrot chopped
- ¾ cup of tomatoes peeled, seeded, and chopped (canned are fine)
- 1 large strip orange zest

INSTRUCTIONS

- Let the navy beans soak for six to eight hours or overnight. After draining, rinse. Please Add them in a pot with 7.5 cm (3 inches) of freshwater covering them. After bringing to a boil, turn off the heat and drain. Reintroduce the beans into the pot, cover with 7.5cm (3 inches) of fresh water, and simmer. After that, simmer for a while on medium-low heat for 30 minutes.
- In the meantime, place a big, heavy skillet over medium-low heat with 1/3 cup of of olive oil. Using a wooden spoon, cook the onion, celery, and carrot for around ten minutes or Before they become soft.
- Include the tomatoes, the sautéed vegetables, and an additional 1/3 cup of of olive oil in the beans. Depending on the age and condition of the beans, simmer the soup for 2 to 2 ½ hours or Before the beans are incredPoundsly soft and the consistency is thick and creamy. Add the orange zest and salt, and cook for about 20 minutes before removing from the fire. Add the remaining olive oil right before turning off the heat.

MUSHROOM BARLEY SOUP RECIPE

Total Time: 45 minutes

INGREDIENTS

- Extra virgin olive oil (I used Private Reserve Greek EVOO)
- 16 Ounces baby bella mushrooms, cleaned well and halved or sliced
- Kosher salt
- 1 yellow onion, chopped
- 4 garlic cloves, chopped
- 2 celery stalks, chopped
- 1 carrot, chopped
- 8 Ounces white mushrooms, cleaned and chopped
- ½ cup of canned crushed tomatoes
- Black pepper
- 1 tsp coriander
- ½ tsp to ¾ tsp smoked paprika
- ½ tsp cumin
- 6 cup ofs of low-sodium broth (vegetable broth or beef broth)
- 1 cup of pearl barley rinsed
- ½ cup of packed chopped parsley

INSTRUCTIONS

- Heat the extra virgin olive. Warm up the oil in a large Dutch pan to a shimmering medium-high heat, but it does not smoke. When the baby bell mushrooms soften and start to take on color, add them and simmer for around five minutes. Take it out of the pot and Add it away for now.
- Add the extra virgin olive oil to the same pot. Add chopped white mushrooms, celery, carrots, onions, and garliCup of Cook for four to five minutes over medium-high heat. Add pepper and salt for seasoning.
- Add the spices (cumin, smoked paprika, and coriander) and crushed tomatoes. Cook, stirring frequently, for about three minutes.

- Add pearl barley and broth. After five minutes of vigorous boiling, reduce the heat. When the barley is soft and cooked thoroughly, about 30 minutes should pass, covered, and simmered over low heat.
- Stir together after adding the cooked bella mushrooms back to the pot. Sauté the mushrooms for around five minutes or Before they are well heated.
- Add some fresh parsley to finish. Spoon into serving bowls and savor!

ITALIAN WHITE BEAN SOUP WITH TUSCAN KALE AND SAUSAGE

Prep Time: 15 Mins | Cook Time:30 Mins | Total Time:45 Mins

INGREDIENTS

- 1½ tbsp olive oil, divided
- 1 pound ground spicy Italian sausage
- 1 yellow onion, diced
- 2 rPoundss celery, diced
- 2 carrots, diced
- 1 tbsp minced garlic
- 1 tsp dried thyme
- ½ tsp dried oregano
- ½ tsp salt, more or less to taste
- ¼ tsp pepper
- 2 (15-ounce cans) cannellini beans, drained and rinsed
- 48 ounces chicken broth (6 cup ofs of)
- 1 (15-ounce can) fire roasted diced tomatoes
- 1 parmesan rind, cut from a block of parmesan cheese
- ½ lemon, juiced
- 3 cup ofs of Tuscan kale, stems reTransferd

INSTRUCTIONS

- The sausage should be browned. Place a big pot or Dutch oven on medium-high heat and cover it. Once heated, add the Italian sausage and ½ tbsp of olive oil to the pot's bottom. With a wooden spoon, shred the sausage as you cook as it browns Before it is no longer pink.

- I don't drain the fat, but if you want to, Transfer the ground sausage to a small Bowl, reserve some grease for the vegetables, and drain any more grease before adding it back to the pot.

- Vegetables are sautéed. When adding the finely chopped onion, carrots, and celery to the saucepan, drizzle with one tbsp of olive oil. Toss in a small tsp of salt. Cook the onion for 6 to 8 minutes or Before it is transparent.

- Let the spices come to life. Add the oregano, thyme, minced garlic, salt, and pepper. Spices should be fragrant after two to three minutes of sautéing.

- Stir in the remaining components. Add the parmesan rind, chicken stock, diced tomatoes roasted over fire, and cannellini beans to the pot.

- Simmer after a boil. Reduce the heat after the soup reaches a boil the heat so that it simmers. For twenty-five minutes, simmer the soup, cover it, and stir now and then.

- Stir in the lemon juice and greens. Stir the greens and lemon juice together after tossing. After the kale has wilted, let the soup simmer uncovered for five minutes. Top with grated Parmesan cheese and serve.

The End

Made in the USA
Las Vegas, NV
08 May 2024

89678632R00079